MW00612906

THE JOY OF
Argument

THE JOY OF
Argument

*91 Ways to Get More of What You Want,
and Less of What You Don't*

Albert Navarra, Esq.

LAW
BOOK
PRESS

Book Design & Production
Columbus Publishing Lab
www.ColumbusPublishingLab.com

Copyright © 2015 by Albert Navarra
LCCN 2015947869

All rights reserved. This book, or parts thereof, may not be reproduced in any
form without permission.

Paperback ISBN 978-1-63337-502-4
E-book ISBN 978-1-63337-050-0

Printed in the United States of America
1 3 5 7 9 10 8 6 4 2

Contents

For Ambu

Preface

THERE ARE THINGS in life you want but will never get unless you learn how to argue for them. And there are things in life you don't want, but you'll get anyway, if you let others persuade you with weak arguments. Here you will learn how to get more of what you want and less of what you don't. You'll learn the joy of argument. Let's get started.

Why Argue?

ERNEST HEMINGWAY SAID, "The world is a fine place and worth fighting for." What does "the world" mean? It could be macro issues, for example, human rights, social and economic policies, and international peace and prosperity. If you care about these issues, they are certainly worth promoting through sound argument. But "the world" can also mean your world, in an individual sense—for example, your health, your work, and your relationships. These issues affect you directly and are worth improving through sound argument. So when you think about it, there are as many reasons to argue as there are reasons to live. Your life itself is an argument, a statement of your beliefs, values, and what is important to you.

You probably argue plenty already, maybe verbally with friends, spouses, children, in-laws, or coworkers, or in writings such as memos, emails, or presentations. Some of your arguments may be long and detailed, others only one sentence long. And others argue with you all the time! Every salesperson or advertisement that tries to sell you something makes an argument. Every politician who seeks your vote makes an argument. A job applicant who wants you to hire him or her makes an argument. A coworker who is trying to solve a problem makes an argument. Leaders who want to inspire make arguments. Hardly a day goes by in your life without an argument of some sort. Argument is simply part of life.

—THE KEY—

Argument is part of life and worth doing well.

An Argument Is Not a Fight

WHEN MANY PEOPLE hear "argument," they think "fight." But the two are not the same. A fight is a battle—for example, a physical altercation or a screaming match. An argument, as used here, is a rational discussion in which you prove a point with reasons. Fights don't provide much joy, but a good argument can. This book focuses on the joy of argument.

—THE KEY—
Argue, but don't fight.

What Good Comes of Argument?

GOOD ARGUMENT IS like fair competition; it makes things better. In a free market economy, market participants compete with each other to provide goods and services to consumers and clients. This competition lowers costs and improves quality. In a society with freedom of speech, a "marketplace of ideas" is created. Anyone can express his or her ideas, opinions, or proposed solutions to problems. Through vigorous and open discussion and debate, the best ideas and opinions prevail, eventually. And society is better off.

Good argument works the same way. A good argument is essentially a rational discussion where you make a point and back it up with relevant reasons. At the end of the day, the better argument should win. So better choices are made and better solutions are implemented.

Bad argument is like unfair competition; it makes things worse. Imagine an economy based on bribery, corruption, and monopoly. Prices skyrocket and quality plummets, along with quality of life. The same thing happens with bad argument. Argument that is irrational, irrelevant, or flawed leads to bad decisions, bad choices, and eventually, bad results. Health, wealth, relationships, and anything else you care about will suffer.

—THE KEY—
Good argument makes things better.

Win at Any Cost?

YOU WILL OCCASIONALLY face the question of right and wrong when arguing. For centuries, the ancient Greeks believed there was a difference between right and wrong and that some things were always right (e.g., "piety," or being religious), and some things were always wrong (e.g., "impiety," or lack of respect for the sacred). These were called objective truths because they were always true, and their truth did not depend on subjective, changing factors such as the personal views of the person arguing, where they lived in the world, or what society or culture they belonged to. Then came the sophists.

The sophists were essentially private tutors, and their services were for hire. Wealthy Athenians would pay sophists to teach their children. The sophists shook things up because they argued there were no objective truths. There was no "right" and "wrong," so when it came to the skill of argument, all that mattered was winning. Aristophanes was writing comedies during this time and described the sophists this way in a play called *The Clouds*: "And if you pay them well, they can teach you how to win a case whether you're in the right or not."

Socrates was also around during this time, and he argued that there were such things as right and wrong, that there were objective, eternal truths. The question for you is whether you follow the sophists or Socrates. Assuming for the moment that you have a choice about what to argue, do you want to win every argument, no matter what, or do you want to get it right?

It feels good to win an argument. It's a feeling of affirmation, that your opinion is important, that you have the power to change things, and that your life matters. It's an existential rush. But should your goal be to win *every* argument? What if you're wrong? All those wonderful feelings of self-fulfillment may fade when you realize the damage you have caused. So consider and appreciate, first, the power you have to influence decisions and change things.

You're in sales, and you convince a customer to buy something they really cannot afford. You win the sales argument, and reap a short-term benefit for yourself or your company. But you harmed the customer because they will suffer financial hardship. Is that what you want? Will the customer do business with you again? Will the customer recommend your company to others?

You're a manager, and you propose a solution to a problem at work. But it's not the best solution; in fact, it's harmful. A coworker had a better idea, but he did not argue as well as you did. So you convinced the company to adopt your idea. You scored a short-term victory. But how long will the celebration last? Your solution will eventually hurt the company. Will the company still think you are a valuable asset to the organization? Will you get a bonus or raise? Will your track record help you obtain employment with another company?

If you fancy yourself a sophist, or you're undecided, consider following Socrates. The pleasure you get from winning an argument for the sake of money, fame, or anything other than the truth is fleeting. Bad decisions lead to bad consequences, which can steal away the very benefit you sought in the first place. Health, wealth, relationships, and anything else you care about will eventually suffer. It's not always clear what is right and what is wrong. Even Socrates never figured it out. But while winning at any cost may bring short-lived fun, the joy of argument, and long-term happiness, comes from trying to get it right, and sometimes doing so.

—THE KEY—
A win "at any cost" may cost you more than you bargained for.

Pick Winners

IF YOU HAVE a choice about which position to take on an issue, think about choosing the better position. Choosing the stronger argument increases your chances of winning the argument. But more than that, better arguments make things better. So the benefits of picking winning arguments are more than a personal victory.

How can you tell which side of an argument is stronger? If there is a stronger argument, you can often identify it during preparation. If you approach the issue objectively, with an open mind, you have a better chance of figuring out which side of the argument is stronger. And if you do this, you already have an advantage: since you have examined the issue from all sides, you are better prepared for counter-attacks! Your open-minded approach strengthens your argument. Sometimes it's hard to tell which side of an issue is superior in any sense. All sides of an argument may seem more or less equally strong. Even so, you will deepen your understanding of the issue by at least trying to pick the winning side during your preparation.

Sometimes you have no choice what to argue. You are told which position to take. For example, salespeople must argue that their employer's product or service is the best choice. Attorneys must advocate their client's position and no other. Although these and similar "representative" roles allow no freedom to choose sides, one hopefully has freedom to choose *how* to make the argument.

—THE KEY—

If you have freedom to choose, try to choose the better argument.

When Not to Argue

ONE OF THE THINGS they teach in self-defense classes is how to avoid trouble in the first place. The same applies to argument. Sometimes it's better not to "engage" an opponent. You've probably had arguments after which you say to yourself, "Wow, I should *never* have brought that up." The trick is anticipating, before you open your mouth, that it's better not to.

There are two things you can do to avoid a good number of regrettable arguments. First, avoid "potholes." Some people have "issues" that are never going to change. So don't try. Maybe your dad isn't very good at complimenting you. Maybe your boss likes to compare you in a negative way to your predecessor. The longer you know someone, the better you know their "potholes." So when you see a pothole, drive around it. Don't argue about it if it's not going to change anything.

Note that *you* have potholes too. So when someone starts talking about one of your sensitive issues, do your best to ignore it.

Don't react emotionally and start an argument that is better avoided. Let there be some awkward silence as you bite your tongue. Change the subject. Move on.

Second, avoid irrational behavior. You can't argue, productively, with a person who is irrational. You can only fight with them, and there's no joy in that. If the other person is not receptive to things like facts and reason, leave it alone. The other person might be going through a difficult time and is just too emotional at the moment to have a rational discussion. Perhaps later, when their situation is calmer, you can have a productive argument.

—The Key—
Know when not to argue.

Look It Up

NOT EVERY ARGUMENT is a matter of opinion. Some arguments are about simple factual questions that can be answered with a little research. Keep alert for these arguments and don't waste too much time debating the issue when you can just Google it. For example, what is the world population? Who was Alexander the Great's father? Which are the ten largest economies?

—THE KEY—
Don't waste time arguing about a simple factual question that you can answer quickly and accurately with a little research.

Get Ready

GREAT ARGUMENTS ARE not accidents. They are the result of great preparation. So get ready.

The very first thing you should do is clarify the main point of the argument. What exactly are you arguing about? What is the issue? What is the disagreement? What do you want to accomplish? What is your point? Or, what is the other person's point?

Second, list the reasons or facts that support your point. Don't go crazy here. Eighteen reasons are too many and will dilute your message and maybe put the other person to sleep. Try to keep the number of reasons to three or four. This may seem like an arbitrarily low number at first, but you have to realize that people can keep only so much new information in their head. They're going to forget most of what you say. So try to focus on a handful of the most important facts or reasons that support your point.

Reasons are critical to good argument. If you don't support your argument with reasons, it's not an argument; it's just a claim. "Jane is a good person to hire" is not an argument. It's just a claim or conclusion. And anybody can make a claim about anything! I can claim that Jane will double company profit. So what! Unless I support my claim with facts or reasons, it's worthless. Lawsuits are similar. You can sue anybody for anything, but unless you have *evidence* to prove your claim, you will lose. If you are rear-ended on the freeway, you can sue the negligent driver for damages, but if you don't provide evidence of damages to your car or your person, you will lose.

"Jane is a good person to hire *because* she is highly educated, has several years experience in this industry, and has been promoted several times by prior employers." Now that's an argument because it makes a point and supports it with reasons or facts. So make "because" your best friend when making an argument. When you make a point, always follow up by saying "because," and then explain your reasons.

When someone else is making an argument and trying to convince you of something, always ask, "Why?" That tiny little word will reveal the reasons or facts that support the other person's point—if there are any! And if there aren't any, you know what to say to that person! So make "why" your best friend when others make arguments to you.

Third, think about what the other person might say during the argument. Remember what Mike Tyson said: "Everyone has a plan until they get punched in the face." Could you be wrong about your point? If so, why? Are you overlooking something? Are your "facts" really true? Is your reasoning flawed? All these considerations are called "counterarguments." Much like anticipating counterpunches, anticipating counterarguments is also critical to your success.

To become really good at anticipating counterarguments you need to be objective. That means looking at your argument without any bias. Think as an independent, neutral decision maker would, like a judge. *Now* how does your argument look? What would a fair, objective judge say about your argument, about your reasons and facts?

To absolutely *master* counterarguments, you need to be more than just objective. You need to learn how to *advocate* your opponent's position. That's right, you need to put yourself in the other person's shoes, or better yet, in the other person's *head*. Only then can you predict and prepare for what the other person might say during the argument. John G. Roberts argued many cases before the United States Supreme Court as an attorney before he became Chief Justice of the Supreme Court. And he was known as one of the best oral advocates *ever*. One reason was his preparation. He would write down hundreds of questions that he might be asked during oral argument, and he would spend hours refining his answers.

Finally, while you are making an argument, you should repeat important points at least a couple of times. Repeating important points helps people understand and remember what's important. It also helps those who are taking notes (you *definitely* want your main points to be in their notes). And it helps to "brand" your argument.

—THE KEY—

Proper preparation prevents poor performance.

The Other Side of the Coin

IF YOU CAN'T see the "other side of the coin," you will probably lose the coin. You must be able to see the issue the way your opponent sees it so you can make your argument stronger. Otherwise, you are blind to weaknesses in your argument and strengths in your opponent's argument.

There are two ways to anticipate what your opponent will say, and thereby "know your enemy." First, the "easy" way: turn your point upside down and argue the exact opposite. If you are arguing that lowering taxes increases job creation, consider the argument that lowering taxes does not increase job creation. How would that argument go? What reasons might someone give in support of that claim? Are they good reasons? Are they weak reasons? If you are trying to convince your spouse to homeschool your child, consider the argument that it is *not* better to homeschool your child. Why might it *not* be better to homeschool? If you are arguing that it is better to rent a copy machine than buy one, consider the argument that it is *not* better to rent than buy. Why might it be better to buy?

So the easy way to play devil's advocate with yourself is to simply argue the *opposite* of your point. Your argument will become stronger because you will be more prepared for what the other person will say.

Then there's the "hard" way to anticipate counterarguments. Try to think of *new* points you have not even thought of yet. Your opponent might say that even if lowering taxes increases jobs, there are other points to consider. Lower tax rates produce less tax revenue. And the new jobs and economic activity might not make up for the decreased tax revenue. So if government spending is not reduced, lower tax rates may increase annual spending deficits and the total national debt. These counterarguments are *new* points that you may not have thought of originally. Maybe you can combine traditional and homeschooling for your child. Maybe it's better to outsource your copy and print jobs rather than do all the work in-house and spend a lot of money renting or buying expensive machines. So outsourcing is a *new* option to consider, besides renting and buying.

I once heard a potential presidential candidate argue that same-sex couples want to marry so that they can have certain rights—for example, property rights and visitation rights—and that it is possible for government to provide those rights without "changing the definition of marriage." But he missed an important counterargument. Same-sex couples also want to be "married." That is, they want society to recognize them as legally married. And this can only be accomplished with same-sex marriage. Whether the potential presidential candidate agreed with same-sex marriage is irrelevant; his argument would have been stronger if he had recognized and addressed the counterargument.

Thinking about new counterpoints will elevate your arguing skills to an extremely high level. This is one of the skills that separate the best arguers from the rest. It will also help you discover alternative solutions to problems. It's not easy, but you should at least try. Push your brain and give yourself some time to anticipate counterpoints and attacks you haven't even thought of yet.

—THE KEY—
Anticipate counterpunches, or get knocked out.

Be Open-Minded

IMPROVING A WEAKNESS increases strength. So if there is a weakness in your argument, you need to know about it. Otherwise, you may get blindsided and lose. So when you prepare, don't act as if the matter is already decided. If you do, you will close your mind to weak spots that can lose the argument for you. Starting your preparation with an open mind can help you

- Identify additional relevant facts that may help or hurt your argument.
- Spot a weakness in your argument.
- Recognize that your opponent has a good point or counter-argument to make.
- Help you find the best response to the other person's argument.
- Strengthen your argument.
- Build trust and confidence.

- Assure everyone that the argument is thorough and addresses everything that is needed; this is particularly important when a lot is at stake.

—THE KEY—

Start with an open mind and you will finish strong.

How to Be Open-Minded in "Closed" Situations

SOMETIMES YOU DON'T have a choice what to argue. Your job requires that you take a certain position. People in sales, advertising, and marketing are paid to promote a particular product or service. They don't have the luxury of switching sides and promoting a competitor's product or service. So you wouldn't want to change your mind in the middle of a sales pitch or argument. People working in a representative capacity have to represent. Imagine a criminal defense attorney having a change of heart during closing arguments and telling the jury the client is guilty!

More than that, your occupation may demand that you continue arguing and give it everything you have, even if you are convinced you will eventually lose! You may be asked by your company to bid on a project, even though you are sure that your bid won't be accepted. You may be asked to solve a problem that you think is utterly hopeless. Nevertheless, undying effort, loyalty, and courage can be quite virtuous—a virtuous act for virtue's sake. And even if you don't see immediate results, there may be positive long-term consequences. The Battle of Thermopylae (between the Persians and the Greeks) was one of the most famous "last stands" in history, and a defeat for the Greeks, but it boosted morale for Greek soldiers in later battles and has inspired many others throughout history.

So if you are required to take a certain position, and hold it until the end, preparation is the time to be open-minded. That's when you want to take an honest look at your argument, opposing arguments, and any new facts that may have popped up. Then make the necessary adjustments to strengthen your argument. Law school professors frequently challenge students to consider an issue from different perspectives. What would the plaintiff argue? What would the defendant argue? What would a court of appeal say? What if you change this fact or that fact? Then what? The interesting thing is that when law students become practicing attorneys, they almost always argue for a particular side or party. But their law school training in being open-minded makes them better advocates for their clients. So when lawyers prepare a case for settlement or trial they try to be open-minded and anticipate counterarguments.

A great salesperson knows as much about competitors' products and services as her own. She's forced to sell her company's stuff. But to prepare, she keeps an open mind that allows her to make a fair assessment of the other options for the customer. And that makes her sales arguments even stronger.

—The Key—

If you are forced to take a particular position, make your argument stronger by keeping an open mind during preparation.

Make It Simple

DON'T EXPECT TO convince anyone one with an argument that is too complicated. Complicated arguments often confuse people. Sometimes they even raise issues of distrust; the other person thinks you may be trying to hide something or mislead them. Or they may think you don't fully understand the situation and that's why you're making it so complicated. Complicated arguments often increase opposition. People get frustrated and say, "Forget it! This is too complicated!"

Some people are impressed by complicated things, especially things they don't understand, so they are more susceptible to over-complicated arguments. A smooth talker can take advantage of this and use a complicated argument with a few buzzwords to convince some of these people. But there's no joy in taking advantage of people. You should also be on guard that you are not persuaded by an argument you don't fully understand.

Masters make it simple. Even if your argument involves many

points and a lot of evidence, you still need to make it simple. No matter how complicated it is (or you think it is), you must simplify. One way to simplify your argument is to write it down in one short sentence. You may think this is impossible, but it can be done. The essence of the most complicated Supreme Court cases in U.S. history can be summarized in a single sentence. So try it. Aim for thirty words or less. That's about the length of a tweet. You should be able to state your main point and reasons in one sentence. Of course, you will expand on your point and reasons during your argument. But you must also be able to *contract* your argument into one sentence during your preparation.

"Cloud computing is the best option for us *because* we'll spend less on hardware and software and have global access to data and programs, 24/7." "We should diversify our investments among stocks, bonds, and real estate *because* different assets perform differently at the same time, so diversifying will give us acceptable gains with less risk." "We should do more aerobic exercise *because* we'll lose weight, increase stamina, strengthen our immune system, reduce tension, and release endorphins, which are natural painkillers."

Next, find someone who knows nothing about your argument, perhaps a friend or relative. If the argument is relatively simple, see if you can persuade the person in two-three minutes. You may think this is impossible. How can I persuade a layperson who knows nothing about my subject? And how can I do it in two minutes? You can at least try by simplifying and being concise. If the argument is more complex, see if you can at least get the person's attention and open his or her mind, again, in a few minutes. Don't tell me you can't do this; try really hard to do it, and see how the effort sharpens your argument.

—THE KEY—

Complicated arguments confuse; simple arguments succeed.

Practice

IF YOUR ARGUMENT is scheduled to happen sometime in the future, then you'll have time to practice. So you should practice. If you lack confidence, you'll probably be eager to practice so that you don't mess up. Fred Astaire was a virtuoso dancer, but not particularly confident. So he practiced, a lot, and it paid off. If you are especially confident, you might decide you don't need practice. But you should practice too. You've nothing to lose by practicing. And you'll probably end up being even more confident!

So what should you practice? Everything. If your presentation is limited to a certain number of minutes, practice to make sure you can finish in time. Record yourself to make sure you speak clearly and at a comfortable rate of speed, not too fast or slow. If you have a video camera, record yourself to see how you look. You should look alive and keenly interested in your *audience*; that will make your audience interested in *you*. Keep your head up, look at the imaginary people you are speaking to, and use hand gestures to emphasize important points.

Also practice making your points and explaining your reasons. Arguments often have parts that are complicated, boring, or just not very persuasive. Work on these parts to make them simpler, more interesting, and more persuasive.

You can also test your argument with friends and associates to get feedback. Your test audience may point out a new counterargument that you hadn't thought of, allowing you to be even better prepared.

Some arguments happen out of the blue, so you won't have time to practice. Or will you? You might not have time to write things down, record yourself, or test your argument with others. But you can still do a "flash preparation." And you can do this even in a few seconds if you need to. Yes you can! First, take a deep breath and relax. Then ask yourself three things: (1) What is your point? (2) Why should anyone believe you? (3) Why would anyone disagree with you? Just thinking about these three questions, even for a very short period of time, will make you better prepared.

—THE KEY—

Things happen during arguments, but the more you prepare and practice, the fewer surprises you will face, and the better you will perform.

Nerves

SOME PEOPLE HAVE preternatural confidence, even if they're not preternaturally competent. They seem able to do anything, even for the first time, without being nervous. They're not nervous making an argument anywhere, anytime, even before a large or important audience. Good for them. Most people will feel nervous, at least a little, before making an argument or presentation. Many will feel so nervous that they worry it may affect their performance. But there are a few things you can do to manage nerves and limit their effect on your performance or argument.

The first thing you must do is prepare, a lot. If you are not adequately prepared, you *should* be nervous! It is often the case that nobody in the audience had the time to prepare on the subject as much as you. So you should seize the opportunity to be the most prepared person in the room on the points you plan to make. This will boost your confidence, and perhaps even make you eager to get out there and make your case.

It's also a good idea to memorize the first two sentences you plan to say. Memorize them word for word. That way you don't have to think too much at the start, when nervousness may be the greatest.

Remember also that nervousness diminishes after a minute or so. Even if your argument is horrible, your nervousness will quickly subside and be replaced by anger at yourself for doing so poorly.

Also keep in mind that you are arguing to *help* someone understand your points and believe them. You're not there simply to look and sound good. Of course you want to look and sound good, but that's not your primary goal. Your primary goal is in the other person's head; help them understand and believe. If they understand and believe, then and only then will you come out looking good. So when you are battling nerves, don't think about yourself and how you are doing; focus on your audience and how *they* are doing. Look at them, sitting there or standing, whatever they are doing. Are they looking at you? No? Then speak louder, right at that guy who's checking his phone. Get his attention. Are they listening, or just staring at you like zombies? Raise your voice a little. Engage them. Never give up on your audience. Never give up on your primary goal, to help them understand your argument.

You should also eat a healthy meal and get a full night's sleep so you don't pass out during your argument. General Thomas Ewing fainted during oral argument before the U.S. Supreme Court, forty years after his father fainted during oral argument before the Court!

—THE KEY—
Focus on your audience, not on yourself.

Speak, Don't Read

HAVE YOU EVER listened to talk radio and heard a caller who was reading what they wanted to say, rather than speaking naturally? It's unmistakable. People sound different when they're reading. Their voices sound wooden, controlled, and less lively. Some radio hosts let it go because they understand that callers get nervous and it's easier for them to read. But I've heard other hosts tell the caller, "Stop reading! Just talk to me!" The U.S. Supreme Court addresses this issue in Supreme Court Rule 28: "Oral argument read from a prepared text is not favored." Reading is a terrible way of arguing. It's okay to be nervous. But you should know your argument well enough so that you don't need to depend on a text for every word. If you don't understand your argument well enough to speak it from memory, you discourage others from making the effort to understand it.

So how do you wean yourself off of reading your arguments? First, you don't have to say every word of your argument perfectly. You're not reciting a poem. You're trying to make a point and back it up with reasons. So you need to cut yourself a little slack and allow for some fumbled words, a few umms and ahhs, and an occasional grammar error. It's okay! A few minor mistakes like these will not kill your argument. But sounding like a robot sure will. So be human, and feel free to err.

Second, instead of trying to memorize an entire argument, word for word, just memorize the points you want to make and the reasons to back up each point. Make a short checklist that fits on one page. For example, if you are trying to convince the marketing and sales director to highlight three points in a marketing and sales campaign, list each point. Remembering three points is not difficult, and even if you get lost during your presentation you can glance at your notes, see the next point, and carry on.

Next, list the key reasons that support each point. Abbreviate your notes. These do not need to be complete sentences. These are just notes to trigger your memory in case you forget. Underline key words, terms, or numbers that you want to emphasize. For example, if your first point is that the company should advertise free shipping, key reasons that support this point may be that it:

- Encourages customers to buy, because they see shipping as an "extra" cost and don't like paying for it.
- Encourages customers to buy, because they don't have to drive to a store to buy.
- Gives our company an advantage over competitors that charge for shipping.
- We can increase prices a little to recover some or all of shipping costs.

—The Key—

Put your points and key reasons on one piece of paper, practice, and speak to your audience; don't read.

Look Alive!

EMOTIONS CAN MAKE or break an argument. If you don't show enough passion, people think you're a robot. If you show too much, people think you're nuts. Either way, your power to persuade decreases. You need to find the sweet spot in between. Be passionate and excited about the merits of your argument. And show your passion. Show you care deeply about what you are arguing for. Show you *believe* in the argument. If you don't care, why should anyone else? But don't lose your head and become irrational. Emotions should fuel your argument, not drive it. It's the wind behind your sails, not the captain of the ship.

First, use your voice to *highlight* important points or facts. How do you highlight a word or sentence? Say it slowly, or a little louder, or with a different accent or inflection. Use your personality here. Loosen up. The point is to vary the volume and tone of your voice to suit what you are saying, to suit your audience, and to avoid sounding like a cheap GPS voice.

Next, use your body to accent what you are saying. Use your hands or arms to emphasize important points. If you are stiff as a board you make it hard for people to concentrate on what you are saying.

Also, make eye contact. Don't stare relentlessly at the other person. That's a little weird. But do make eye contact to show the other person you are paying attention to them.

If you are speaking to a group of people, look at several of them. Again, don't force it. You don't have to look from person to person until you've covered everyone in the room. Let it happen naturally. You'll find that you will get to know the audience better as you look into their eyes. You'll get a sense of whether they are paying attention, whether they understand, and whether they agree. And your audience will sense that you care about them.

Last, whenever possible, argue in a friendly tone. When appropriate, show genuine love and kindness. The Dalai Lama discusses helping pessimists and worriers by arguing not just with reason, but by also showing genuine love and affection for the person. (*Daily Advice from the Heart*, the Dalai Lama.)

On that note, in the movie *Glengarry Glen Ross*, Blake, a businessman (Alec Baldwin), tries to motivate a room full of real estate salesmen to sell more. There's some profanity, so beware. And I don't recommend that you use profanity in arguments. But the scene is a laundry list of techniques you can use to look alive, without looking crazy. Listen to how Baldwin emphasizes certain words by saying them louder, or softer, or slower. Notice how he repeats certain words (for emphasis), and how he uses the power of pauses. Watch him move about the room and engage each salesperson, *personally.*

But notice that Baldwin never loses it. Not for a second is he crazy. Intense, yes. But completely rational.

—THE KEY—
Look alive without looking crazy.

Listen!

ARGUING WITHOUT LISTENING is like flying without seeing. You won't know where you need to go with your argument. First, if someone is trying to convince you of something, but does not listen to you, will you agree with him or her? Probably not. More likely you'll be irritated that the other person is just talking and not listening. Listening shows the other person you are open-minded, objective, sincere, compassionate, helpful, and trustworthy (*even if you're not!*).

Also, if you do not listen to the other person you might miss important points. Careful listening can reveal answers to these critical questions:

- *Why* does the other person disagree with you?
- After you've argued for a while, why does the other person *still* disagree with you?
- Does the other person *misunderstand* something you are saying?

- Is the other person being *honest* with you about what's important to them?
- What is it going to *take* to persuade the other person?
- Is there a *flaw* in your argument you need to address?
- Is there a flaw in the other person's argument you need to point out?

Also, if you don't shut up and listen patiently, you might overreact to something the other person said that is not very important. So avoid being too reactive, like a rubber ball. It's better to connect and learn what's going on in the other person's head. Then you can process what you've learned, and have a better response. Sales professionals talk about the 70/30 rule: listen 70% of the time, talk 30%. It's a nice rule of thumb that is helpful in any argument, not just sales.

Whether you are trying to convince a company to hire you, convince a client to buy a product or service, or convince a loved one to vacation in Europe rather than Hawaii, you must listen carefully to what the other person is saying (or not saying). Only then will you make the emotional connection that is needed to persuade. Only then will you pick up on logical issues you need to address. And don't stop listening until the argument is over!

—THE KEY—
Careful listening will reveal where you need to go in your argument.

Emotional Intelligence

NO MATTER HOW logical you are, if you mishandle emotions you will not persuade. So you need to pay attention, get a sense of the person's emotional state, and adjust accordingly. For example, if the other person is becoming too emotional, angry, or defensive, then tone it down a little. Speak more softly. Don't hush your voice in a patronizing manner and say *"Caaalllllmmm dooowwwwwnnn."* Just lower your voice a little, and argue your points. Focus on the argument, and respond to counterpoints as needed. This will encourage the other person to eventually calm down and refocus on the argument as well. Also, be patient, and give the other person time to calm down. When an engine overheats, it takes time to cool down. If you made your coffee too hot, it takes time to cool down. So be patient with a person who has become too emotional. If needed, just take a break and pick it up later. You also need to stay calm and resist the temptation to get overly emotional yourself.

If the other person seems bored, apathetic, or disinterested, then you need to inspire! Don't be afraid to raise your voice a little, and vary the tone of your voice to suit what you are saying. Get the other person's attention back, and then refocus on the argument. Emphasize the points that matter the most to the person, and skip the small stuff. Cut to the chase! If the other person is most concerned with cost or other numbers, focus on that. If the prospect is interested in something unique about your product or service, go to that. If you dillydally around with other topics, the prospect will think that your advertised "USP" (unique selling proposition) is just that—advertisement—and not something you take seriously.

If the other person seems insecure, uncertain, or doubtful, then you need to reassure. Speak with confidence. Keep your voice strong. Keep your sentences short. And make points that are reassuring. If you are trying to make a sale, and you sense that the buyer is a little uncertain, emphasize points that minimize risk for the buyer. Perhaps there's a trial period, no fee for ending the contract, no long-term commitment required, or price matching. Perhaps you can start with a smaller order so the buyer can try it out before making a fuller commitment.

Sometimes you will argue with a person who is not as familiar with the subject as you. If they do not understand the argument, they might turn their attention to *you*, and wonder if they can trust you. The other person may become intimidated, shy, or feel overmatched. In this case try to humble yourself. Emphasize objective, measurable facts that the other person can rely on (and confirm with other sources), so the person doesn't feel the need to rely on you. This will help increase the other person's confidence. Take yourself, your personality, or whatever it is that is intimidating the other person out of the picture. This will allow the other person to focus on the argument instead of you. If you are trying to make a sale and the customer is questioning the quality of the product or service, refer them to online reviews, if there are any. If the customer is questioning price, provide resources (perhaps online) for the customer to compare alternatives. If you are arguing about a matter of history, and the other person isn't as familiar with the subject as you are, mention some sources where the person can find more information that will confirm what you are saying.

—THE KEY—

Recognize the other person's emotions, and respond accordingly.

Watch Your Body Language

BODY LANGUAGE IS the way you stand, the way you sit, the way you hold your arms, where you look, the expression on your face, and even the way you breathe. And it's usually involuntary, subconscious, and not planned. It's unfiltered thoughts and feelings. So body language is often more truthful and accurate than spoken language—actions speak louder than words. Because it sends a signal, people read body language as they read traffic signs.

So if the other person is a staggering bore, resist the urge to yawn, stare at an attractive person nearby, slouch, or put your head in your hand. The other person will read your body language, conclude you couldn't care less about what they are saying, and probably not agree with you. If the other person is incredibly ridiculous, don't make funny faces, roll your eyes, flash a condescending smile, shake your head, sigh, or hold your hands up in the air in exasperation. The other person will likely find your body language to be insulting. Even a *hint* of negative body language can make the other person feel that you are apathetic, dismissive, arrogant, or insulting. In addition to sending all the wrong signals, bad body language distracts the other person's attention from your argument, your points, your reasons, and everything that you *want* the person to think about.

Good body language shows you are interested, open-minded, and respectful, even if you disagree. Look the other person in the eye. Sit up straight or stand straight, whichever is appropriate for the setting. Keep your arms unfolded and your hands open. Breathe normally. Smile when appropriate. And never insult.

I read an article about a retired homicide detective who was famously good at getting suspects to confess. He said the most important thing was gaining the person's confidence and respect. The same applies to argument. If you can gain the other person's confidence and respect, you will have an easier time persuading that person. The right body language can help.

—THE KEY—
Send the right signals with good body language.

Reading Minds and Hearts

AS YOU TRY to persuade people, wouldn't you like to know what they are thinking or feeling? Are they interested? Do they understand what you are saying? Are they agreeing with you? You can get some insight into these things if you can read their body language. This is part of emotional intelligence, and it will help you argue and persuade. Here is a short list of the most common body language and what it may indicate.

- Leaning back in a chair may indicate confidence, arrogance, or sometimes laziness. A confident or arrogant person may not have an open mind, and a lazy person doesn't even care. So focus on the parts of your argument that matter the most to the other person, and don't waste time on the small stuff. Get their attention. You may not be able to persuade them immediately, but you can at least get them to think about what you are saying. Maybe later they'll come around to your position.

- Leaning forward in a chair may indicate a person is eager, ready for action, interested, or aggressive. So if you're trying to persuade them, you've got their attention and things may be going well. If the other person is trying to persuade you, don't get too caught up in their enthusiasm; focus on their argument and make sure it makes sense.

- Lack of eye contact may indicate deception or untrustworthiness. But in some cultures, for example Asia and Latin America, direct eye contact may seem disrespectful or too aggressive. Staring relentlessly may indicate aggressiveness; avoid doing this or being intimidated by someone who does this to you.

- Hands on the hips may indicate a person is ready for action, aggressive, or sizing you up. In any case, you've got their attention; make the most of it.

- Crossing or folding arms may indicate a person is defensive, resistant, or uncomfortable (or just trying to keep warm). Try to figure out what the problem is. If you can, do your best to smooth it out. If you can't smooth it out, emphasize something positive. Stay positive and don't get too discouraged.

- Fidgeting or fussing with clothes may indicate a person is nervous or disapproves. Handle this the same as crossing or folding arms.

- Looking at a phone or watch may indicate boredom or lack of interest. Get their attention, as you do with a person who is leaning back.

- Chin up high, looking down their nose at you, may indicate defiance or superiority. This person may be close-minded. Handle them the same as leaning back in a chair.
- Tilting the head to the side may indicate interest. So you've got their attention.
- Mirroring or synchronicity is when the other person's body language matches yours. You lean forward and so do they. You tilt your head and so do they. This may indicate good rapport and agreement.

—THE KEY—

Read body language and respond appropriately.

Laugh Carefully

SOMETIMES THE PERSON you are arguing with wants to distract you, so they decide to crack a joke and make you laugh. You might also be tempted to do this sometimes. Maybe your argument isn't going so well, so you say something funny to loosen things up a little. A little humor isn't the end of the world. But don't allow humor to steal the show, and distract from what really matters. The other person may be funny, but are they right?

—THE KEY—
Don't make a joke out of the argument.

"Improvise, Adapt and Overcome"
(Unofficial Mantra of the U.S. Marine Corps)

NO MATTER HOW much you prepare, unexpected things happen during argument. New facts emerge and surprising points are made. So you need to improvise, adapt, and overcome. In general, if something comes up that hurts your argument, stay calm. Don't blurt out a response just for the sake of saying something. Stay loose. Think. Reflect. A moment of calm, silent thought can be extraordinarily powerful and bring outstanding results. You may just think of something important to say, if you keep your mind calm. It also shows the other person that you are thoughtful, open-minded, and objective—not emotional, stubborn, and biased.

If someone points out a weakness in your argument, consider whether it is a fatal weakness. If the weakness does not totally destroy your argument, and you don't have a good response, it's okay to admit your argument has a weakness and keep arguing. Most arguments have weaknesses and do not need to be perfect to be sound and persuasive. Consider "opportunity cost," for example. If you make a

choice between several options, you will not enjoy the potential benefit from the option that you do not choose. That's the "cost" of making
a choice. For example, if you are on vacation and you have enough
time and money to visit only one city, you have to choose one city.
You won't enjoy the benefit of seeing a city you did not choose to
see; that's the opportunity "cost." It's not a perfect situation, but that
doesn't mean that you made the wrong choice. The same applies to
arguments. An argument can still be sound and persuasive even it it's
not perfect.

If you suddenly recognize a strength in your *opponent's* argument, consider whether it's "game over" for you. If it's not, sometimes
you can admit that your opponent has a good point and still carry on
your argument. If you are confronted with new facts, first make sure
they are really true. There's no need to concede a point unless you're
sure it's true. And even if it is true, put it in context. Are other facts
(that support your argument) more important? If part of your argument doesn't seem to hold up rationally, it's okay to admit it. Maybe
you don't have all the facts you need to support your point. Maybe
there's a flaw in your reasoning. Whatever the case, it's okay to admit
that your argument is weak in some respect. You're just being honest,
objective, and rational. Your only alternative is to deny reality and
make yourself appear biased and irrational; how will that help you?

But if you admit a weakness, you don't have to give up all hope.
Such honesty, by itself, is sometimes enough to win over the other
side. Being candid and admitting a weakness can be very disarming.
It sometimes leads to agreement or a better result. I had a case, as a
defense attorney, in which I admitted to the opposing attorney that
I had no defenses. None. The attorney was apparently moved by my

candid admission and agreed to settle the case and give my client a 40% discount, saving my client a lot of money.

If you're listening carefully, you might also catch the other person unwittingly mentioning a new fact that helps your argument. If it's an important fact, mention it. Don't gloat about it, of course. Just point it out. The other person might also make an important misstatement. Misstatements can be intentional, negligent, or accidental. Regardless, keep the record straight. Do not let a misstatement distort the argument.

It's also important to adapt to reasons why the other person *still* doesn't agree with you. After you've made your case, why does the other person still disagree? You need to know the reason so you can address it. Their reasons for disagreement might even change, so pay attention during the argument. As you learn these things, improvise, adapt and overcome. Failure to do so means failure.

—THE KEY—
Improvise, adapt, and overcome the unexpected.

What Are We Arguing About?

IT'S COMMON AT the beginning of an argument for each side to quickly blurt out several points. Each side feels passionately about the subject. A little adrenaline kicks in. Next thing you know, a whole bunch of topics are on the table. Sometimes one sentence contains several separate points! A discussion can become a sloppy mess in a hurry.

So clarify, calmly, what you are arguing about. If you want to tackle several topics, then clarify which topic you want to discuss first. And make sure the other person agrees on which topic you are arguing about. It's common for one person to argue one issue while the other person keeps arguing about something completely different (or keeps *thinking* about a different topic while they stare blankly at you). If the other person won't concentrate on the point you want to discuss first, consider discussing the point they are so hung up on, then moving on to your point when they seem ready.

Try as you might, arguments still go astray sometimes. You

will find yourself arguing about things you never dreamed of. Take a breath, and clarify what you are arguing about. Get back to the original question, and do your best to resolve it. Then move on to the next topic, if there is one.

—The Key—

Clarify, and if necessary, clarify again what you are arguing about.

One Thing at a Time

YOU ARE ARGUING about one topic when something else comes to mind. And you're very tempted to bring it up. But if you do, you risk confusing, distracting, or frustrating the other person. So it's better to argue like a surgeon; focus on one area at a time, and seek closure for each point. Closure is agreement, or clear understanding why there is no agreement. So when you feel tempted to jump to another topic, stay on point. Focus. And close. Then, if you think it's wise, you can move on to the other topic.

The same holds true when someone is arguing with you and jumping from topic to topic. Calmly bring their attention back to the original topic and seek closure (agreement, or clear understanding why there is no agreement).

You are running a meeting and you have to decide several questions during the meeting. But if every topic is on the table at the same time, the meeting will resemble a food fight. So it's better to make it like a five-star lunch buffet. Each topic in its own little space. One topic at a time, focus, and close.

Arguing one thing at a time may also eliminate the need to argue other points. You and your partner are trying to decide *where* to vacation, *when* to vacation, and whether to take your *kids*. That's *three* different points. Quite a handful. But if you decide one question, the other questions might get easier. For example, if you decide to take your kids and they are in school during spring and fall, then you know when to pack—summer!

Many arguments are not resolved in one go. So if you and the other person cannot agree on a point, but you have clarified why you don't agree, you can revisit the subject another day and pick up where you left off. Maybe by then more information will be available and you can resolve the issue.

—THE KEY—
Stay on point until you agree
or understand clearly why you don't agree.

Say Things That Matter

TO REALIZE THE joy of argument and all the wonderful things it can bring, you need to think about and say things that *matter*. Don't just say things because it feels good to say them. Say things because they are relevant and help prove your point.

Start by arguing relevant facts. And spend most of your time on the *most* relevant facts. A fact is relevant if it tends to prove your point; these are the facts you emphasize when you are proving a point. For example, let's say you argue that there is an economic recession. Relevant facts would be decreased income levels, decreased gross domestic product (GDP), decreased consumer spending, and increased unemployment. These facts, if true, would tend to prove your point.

But before you declare victory, keep in mind that a fact is also relevant if it tends to *disprove* your point; these are the facts your opponent emphasizes when he tries to prove you wrong. Increased income levels, increased gross domestic product, increased consumer spending, and decreased unemployment, if true, would tend to disprove your point. These facts make up the "other side of the coin," and you should be aware of them if they are true.

So it's important to identify the relevant facts in an argument. But it's not enough to simply argue relevant facts. To persuade, you need to argue the *most* relevant facts. Let's say you and a friend are arguing about whether there is an economic recession. Your friend says "I just came back from Dubai. The business-class lounge was packed. The plane was completely full. Where's the recession? I don't see any recession!" Is it relevant that the business lounge in Dubai International Airport is full? Sure, a busy airport is a sign of economic activity. But is this the *most* important fact as to whether there is a recession? Probably not. First, airports tend to attract people with money, so an airport is not always the best barometer of general economic conditions. Second, airlines have been running their planes fuller in recent years because of consolidation, partnerships, elimination of unprofitable routes, technology, and fuel costs. And many seats are taken by off-duty airline staff and passengers using frequent-flier miles. These factors don't tend to indicate the end of a recession. So the *most* relevant facts in this argument are probably broader economic statistics, for example income levels, unemployment, GDP, and consumer spending (a tiny fraction of which would be found in the business lounge).

I once overheard a woman say to another woman, "Can I ask what was the problem with you and your husband? Not to poke in your personal matters. Just to get an insight to help with mine." It's hard to imagine how insight into one random marriage can provide insight into another marriage. There are too many variables between relationships. If the woman wanted to better understand issues with her marriage, the best source of information would be her and her husband. And for assistance in analyzing things, perhaps a qualified professional could help. But information about a random marriage simply doesn't matter.

The most common flaw in bad arguments is saying stuff that is not relevant. Most bad reasoning comes down to saying things that don't prove, or even tend to prove, the point. Say things that matter, and especially the things that matter *most*, and you stand a much better chance of persuading.

—THE KEY—
Focus on the facts that matter the *most*.

Ignore Things That Don't Matter

WHEN YOU THINK about your argument, you may realize there is a universe of information that is completely irrelevant to your argument. So an important part of good reasoning is ferreting out facts and points that may initially seem relevant or enticing, but in reality do not matter one bit. Trying to persuade by attacking the other person personally, by appealing to what "most" other people think, or by instilling fear are a few of many examples of irrelevancy that we will cover in this book. In essence, discussing things that are irrelevant to an argument is the same as changing the subject of the argument and arguing about something else.

With practice you can develop a very sensitive "radar" for things that don't matter. Your "relevancy radar" will help you defend yourself against irrelevant information. And it will help you avoid wasting time and effort arguing irrelevant points.

—The Key—

Don't be distracted, discouraged, or persuaded
by the infinite number of things that simply don't matter.

Show Me the Facts!

ONE DAY I took the train. I like to read on trains so I bought three newspapers. First, I read a front page article in USA Today called "White House Slow to Regulate: Economy, Election Put the Brakes on Pace to Issue Rules." The article argued that the Obama administration was issuing fewer regulations because of possible negative effects on the faltering economy and the 2012 elections. But the article said virtually nothing about which proposed regulations the administration was putting on hold. The article merely mentioned rules "to protect the food supply, reduce exposure to silica dust, and require rear-view cameras or other devices on cars." Protect the food supply, *how*? Reduce silica dust, *where*? Require *what* "other devices" on cars? What can anyone say about the administration if one doesn't even know what the proposed rules are? And the article said nothing about how these or other proposed rules would supposedly affect the economy or election.

After reading that fact-devoid article I felt a little peckish, so I visited the dining car for a coconut yogurt with little crunchy balls of chocolate. Then I read a full-page interview of a Yale Professor in the Wall Street Journal called "The Empire Strikes Back." The professor argued that the U.S. is no longer battling for democracy and international order. But the interview hardly mentioned the Obama administration's foreign policy record. The interview referred only to "the Obama administration's desire to lead from behind and seek United Nations approval for actions abroad," "President Obama's foreign policy," and "The conduct of the Obama administration." The interview managed to discuss the Chinese, Mughal, Persian, Roman, Mayan and Ottoman empires, the Thirty Years' War, 19th century Britain, the Treaty of Westphalia, the Congress of Vienna in 1814, World Wars I and II, and even Charles Dickens. So I think there was room in this interview for a few more facts regarding the Obama administration's foreign policies. How can one judge the administration without knowing what it has done?

Last, I read a commentary in the International Herald Tribune called "Mitt's Olympic Meddle." The author criticized Republican presidential contender Mitt Romney for blurting out during a TV interview "a shockingly ill-considered, if undeniably true, observation" about the 2012 London Olympics. The author concluded that Romney is "removed, always struggling to connect and emote," and questioned whether Romney is the best choice for president. Missing from the commentary was what Romney *said!* Would you mind telling us, *please*? Can you trust the readers with that fact? Can we be free to judge for ourselves how "shocking" or "ill-considered" Romney's statement was, and how it reflects on Romney's fitness for the office of president? This also was a long, three-column commentary, so there was plenty of space to work with.

—The Key—

An opinion is only as strong as the facts upon which it is based;
so show the facts.

What Will Victory Look Like?

EVERY ARGUMENT MAKES a point (conclusion) and backs it up with reasons. There are two main ways to do this: deductive and inductive. In a deductive argument, if the reasons that support the point are true, and there's a connection between the reasons and the conclusion, then the conclusion *must* be true. The result is an absolute *certainty*. Here's an example:

> Reason 1: Exercise causes good health.
> Reason 2: Good health causes happiness.
> **Conclusion**: Exercise causes happiness.

If reasons one and two are true, the conclusion must be true. It's not just *probably* true—it's *definitely* true. Here's another example.

> Reason 1: *Education* increases economic *opportunities*.
> Reason 2: Increasing economic *opportunities* increases *wealth*.
> **Conclusion**: *Education* increases *wealth*.

I've highlighted the terms that connect the reasons and the conclusion; you can see how the first reason leads to the second, and how the conclusion follows from both reasons. So if the reasons are true, then the conclusion absolutely must be true. It's a certainty.

Deductive arguments are very common in logic books and very rare in real life. So you will rarely be able to prove your point with certainty. In most cases, "victory" will not be conclusive proof, or a 100% certainty.

Inductive arguments, on the other hand, are the bread and butter of daily life. They are by far the most common form of argument you will make and others will present to you. And with practice they are relatively easy to put together and assess. The catch is that they do not produce certainty. If the reasons are true, and relevant, the conclusion will *probably* be true, but it's not absolutely *certain* that the conclusion will be true. Here's an example:

Reason 1: Mira exercises daily.
Reason 2: Mira sleeps 8 hours a day.
Reason 3: Mira eats a healthy diet.
Reason 4: Mira has very little stress.
Conclusion: Mira is happy.

You can see that if reasons one through four are true, the conclusion is *probably* true. But the conclusion is not *necessarily* true. It is possible that Mira is still not happy, despite doing all these things. It's the old, "If it looks like a duck, and walks like a duck, then it's a duck" argument. Look at the number of reasons given, and how relevant they are. The more reasons there are, and the more relevant they are, the higher the degree of probability that the conclusion is true. Here's another example.

Reason 1: Mira exercises daily.
Reason 2: Mira sleeps eight hours a day.
Reason 3: Mira eats a healthy diet.
Reason 4: Mira has very little stress.
Conclusion: Mira is wealthy.

First, is this argument deductive (certainty) or inductive (probability)? If the reasons are true, the conclusion is not *necessarily* true. So if you said inductive, you're correct. So we know that, at best, we'll end up with some degree of probability, but not a certainty.

Next, would you say that the conclusion is probably true? I wouldn't. Even if all the reasons are true, they are not very relevant to the conclusion. The reasons don't "point" to the conclusion, or indicate the conclusion is true. The conclusion might be true, but the likelihood is very low.

—THE KEY—
Consider whether the argument will provide certainty (rare)
or just a probability (common).

Predictions

LIFE HAS FEW certainties. Mostly, we deal with probabilities. So the question is usually not whether something is certain, but whether it is probable. Instead of "knowing" things, we (essentially) make predictions. For example, is one diet better than another? Will a particular college major lead to a lucrative career? Will a job candidate be a good employee? Will a particular investment be profitable? Will your fiancé be a good spouse or parent? When you make these decisions and most others that life presents, you end up with some degree of probability: not likely, likely, or very likely. In most cases, this is the best we can do.

Precision may not possible, but you can think in terms of percentages. If there is less than a 10% chance that something is true, then it is highly unlikely. Less than a 50% chance means it is not likely, or not probable. More than a 50% chance means it is likely, or probable. More than a 90% chance means it is very likely.

The question is, how do you judge how probable something is?

Whether you are making the argument, or someone else is trying to persuade you, you'll want to make that judgment as accurately as possible. In a way, it's like predicting the future. The more facts you have, the more accurate your judgment will be. Imagine a jigsaw puzzle with 1,000 pieces. You don't know what the picture is. You are shown just *one* piece. Can you say what the picture is? Highly unlikely! You need more pieces. If you have 999 pieces, can you say what the picture is? Very likely! That's how most arguments work. The more information you have, the better your judgment.

Is it a duck? If the only fact you have is that it sounds like a duck, it could just be someone using a duck call. If you can see it, and it looks and sounds like a duck, it's more likely a duck. But it could be a decoy, and someone could be using a duck call nearby! If it looks like a duck, sounds like a duck, and moves like a duck, it's even more likely a duck. But there is still no *certainty*. Someone could be using a duck call, and you could be looking at a battery-operated decoy "robo-duck"! These things have moving wings and even dive into the water like real ducks! Nevertheless, the more facts you have, the more accurate your judgment will be.

If you meet a job candidate only once, date a person only a few weeks, or have very limited information or facts, how accurate will your judgment be? Not very. If you want to "predict" the future, then get as many facts or "pieces of the puzzle" as possible.

—THE KEY—
The more facts or information you have,
the more accurate your judgment will be.

"Yes or No" Questions

YES OR NO questions can clarify and focus an argument in a hurry. This can be a good thing. You might be surprised to learn the other person actually agrees with you! But yes or no questions are also very direct and blunt, so they can also end discussions, sometimes prematurely. So be sure it's the right time and place before asking a yes or no question.

As a rule of thumb, ask a yes or no question if you need to clarify something and there's not much harm in asking. For example, let's say you have presented several possible solutions to a problem. And you think these are the only options worth considering. But you're not sure whether the other person agrees these are the only options. Maybe they think there's another option that you haven't considered. You need clarity. So you can ask, "Do you agree these are the only options?" There's not much downside risk to a yes or no question here. If the person says no, and offers another option, you can explore that new option. Nor does asking a yes or no question here make the person feel pressured or on the defensive. Instead, they probably feel respected and reassured that the argument is fair and thorough.

Different situation. You offer a reason in support of your argument. But you're not sure if the other person thinks it's relevant. Ask, so you can have clarity. You're not asking if he agrees with your *entire* argument; you're asking only if the person thinks something is worth considering. Again, there's little downside risk in asking. Similarly, if you offer a fact in support of your argument but you're not sure the other person thinks the fact is true, ask. You at least need to know if they think a fact is true or not. If they're honest, they'll tell you what they think.

Now let's say you're making a sales argument and you just met the potential buyer. If you *start* the discussion with a yes or no question, for example, "Can I write it up?" or "Do you like it?" you might get a quick "No." Discussion over. So it's better to spend some time building rapport and making your argument (main points, main reasons). For example, a real estate agent would not want to ask a buyer if he likes the condominium five minutes after showing the property. A "no" answer could kill the sale immediately. Instead, the agent may want to ask more basic, fundamental questions. For example, "This property has a lot of natural sunlight. Is that important to you?" "This property has only one community wall with a neighbor. Is privacy and quiet important?" These yes or no questions will bring clarity by revealing whether factors like sunlight and privacy are *relevant* to the buyer.

You prepared extensively for a negotiation. During the negotiation, you're paying close attention to the other person and you notice that he is not as prepared as you are. If you ask a "bottom line" yes or no question too early (e.g., "Do you agree to this amount?"), the other person may become defensive and draw a "line in the sand." It's their way of compensating for their lack of preparation. A better approach would be to make your argument first (main points and reasons). Give the other person a chance to understand why they should agree before simply asking if they do.

If you are dealing with someone who is unprepared and at a disadvantage to you, you may even want to mention an argument that the other person would make if they *were* prepared. You can, for a moment, take their position. Then rebut "their" argument and show that your position is better. This approach can be both disarming and reassuring to the other person, as you demonstrate that you know not only your stuff, but you know their stuff too! The other person becomes more likely to agree with you (a form of reciprocation?) as they learn that the argument is fair and that all sides are being considered.

—The Key—

Ask a yes or no question when it can bring clarity you need, without much downside risk.

Ask Why

IF YOU'VE ARGUED with a person for a while, and they still don't agree with you, you need to know why. So if you don't already know, ask. That way you can focus on points that will persuade, rather than waste time and effort on points the other person already agrees on or doesn't care about.

There might be only one reason the other person doesn't yet agree, or there may be several. Their reasons may be purely emotional, completely logical, or both. So ask. "Why do you disagree?" If you want to be subtler, you can rephrase. "Are there any objections to . . ." "Are there any obstacles to . . ."

You can also be more specific with your questions. "Why do you think that particular fact matters?" "Why do you think this fact is not relevant?" "Do you think it matters that. . . ." "Do you think it's important that. . . ." "Why don't you think this fact is true?"

Sometimes the other person is not completely honest about why they disagree with you. They have hidden reasons. If you think some gentle prodding will bring it out, ask. "Are there any other issues that you're thinking about?" "Do you have any other concerns that we should consider?" "Am I covering everything that matters to you?" "I just want to be thorough."

—The Key—

Find out exactly what the hang-up is so you can address it.

Argue by Asking

IT MAY SEEM STRANGE, but you can carry on an entire argument and accomplish your goal by just asking questions. The Greek philosopher Socrates did it all the time, and he was one of the best at making a convincing argument. In fact, the "Socratic Method," a form of argument based on asking and answering questions, is still used today in most American law schools. If all you do is say one thing after another, one point after another, without ever asking the other person a question, how do you think the other person will feel? The person will probably feel ignored, unimportant, and like an inferior who's supposed to just agree with you when you eventually stop talking.

Ask questions, and the other person feels important, respected, and empowered. And when the other person answers, they may end up convincing themselves! So consider "arguing by asking" when you catch yourself talking too much. If the other person is tuning out because you're talking too much, reengage them by asking a question. Also consider "arguing by asking" when you don't understand the other person's argument. Ask questions to clarify points, clarify facts, and flesh out the nature of the disagreement. There may come a point when you have no idea why the other person disagrees with you. You've made your best pitch but they're still not budging. Ask why. Identify the hurdles so you can overcome them.

Asking questions may make you feel a little vulnerable. There's a sense that you are giving up control of the discussion, and there's also the risk of what the person might say if you give them a chance to talk! But you should trust your argument and preparation, and your ability to handle whatever the person says in a thoughtful, sincere, and courteous manner. Asking questions is very powerful. It's disarming and it builds trust by creating an impression of objectivity, teamwork, and joint effort.

—The Key—
Arguing by asking can be a disarming way
of providing clarity and agreement.

Don't Play Dominoes

ON APRIL 7, 1954, President Dwight D. Eisenhower gave a news conference. The sixth question was by Robert Richards, Copley Press: *"Mr. President, would you mind commenting on the strategic importance of Indochina to the free world?"*

The President gave one of the most famous (and in the aftermath of the Vietnam war, most consequential) "domino" arguments ever presented:

> *"[Y]ou have broader considerations that might follow what you would call the 'falling domino' principle. You have a row of dominoes set up, you knock over the first one, and what will happen to the last one is the certainty that it will go over very quickly."*

> *"[W]hen we come to the possible sequence of events, the loss of Indochina, of Burma, of Thailand, of the*

*Peninsula, and Indonesia following, now you be-
gin to talk about areas that not only multiply the
disadvantages that you would suffer through loss
of materials, sources of materials, but now you are
talking really about millions and millions and millions of people."*

The President was arguing that if we let the Communists take
over Vietnam, then other countries in the region would fall to Communist rule, one by one, just like dominoes. It's a powerful visual—
one domino knocking down another, then another, and so on. And
the President added the word "certainty" in the second sentence for its
persuasive effect. But countries aren't dominoes. Dominoes fall pre-
dictably because of laws of physics and gravity—laws that countries
don't follow. So it is not entirely "certain" how events in one country
will affect another country.

You want to give your child a smart phone. But your partner
says if you do, then the child will play games on the phone, study less,
and get lower grades. Basically a smart phone will cause grades to fall,
just like dominoes. But must it be so? If you don't want your child
playing any games, you could remove all games from the phone. Or
you could allow some gaming but also ensure that study time is not
decreased. If managed well, it's not certain or even likely that a smart
phone will eventually cause lower grades. All the dominoes need not
fall.

When government proposes a new law to achieve a specific goal,
particularly in an area that has been essentially unregulated (e.g., the
Internet), one might express the concern that if the new law passes,

government won't stop with one law; they'll continue to regulate the area with overly burdensome rules and regulations. "Give them an inch and they'll take a mile." But it is not a certainty that the government will follow a new law with any particular regulations in the future. Any new regulations would need to be investigated, proposed, debated, and approved by the relevant government agency. They don't happen automatically, like falling dominoes. And if fear of possible future regulations is enough to stop a proposed new law, then no new laws would pass. Government would be impotent, unable to address various social and economic problems.

When someone makes a domino argument, ask for reasons or evidence why the next "domino" will fall. Otherwise, a domino argument is just speculation.

—THE KEY—
Only dominoes fall like dominoes.

Are the Numbers Accurate?

STATISTICS CAN BE very persuasive because they're *measurable*. They create a sense of objectivity because they're based on math. Two plus two equals four. Who can argue with that? So people cite numbers for everything you can imagine. The number of illegal immigrants, the number of people without health insurance, the number of people unemployed, and so on. But sometimes people cite numbers that are not accurate. Or it's unclear exactly what the numbers measure. So sometimes numbers don't live up to the hype. I once heard a political consultant state, authoritatively, that political action committees affiliated with the opposing party have spent "hundreds of millions of dollars" on behalf of candidates without disclosing the donations to the Federal Election Committee. Sounds pretty bad, doesn't it? But wait a minute. How does the consultant know the figure is *"hundreds of millions"* of dollars? Where's the *evidence* for that? Especially if the donations were not disclosed! If donations were not disclosed, how can anyone know the amounts?

Author Sam Harris created some controversy in 2014 when he appeared on Bill Maher's HBO show, "Real Time," and said that about 20% of Muslims are either jihadists or Islamists who want to force their interpretation of Islam on the rest of society. Harris later appeared on CNN's Fareed Zakaria GPS, where Zakaria questioned the figure of 20%. Harris explained there's a difference between a jihadist and an Islamist, but that he had grouped them together. In that case, Harris could have avoided confusion by not grouping jihadists and Islamists together in the figure of 20%.

—THE KEY—
Dig to find out what the number really measures,
and if it's reasonably accurate.

What Do the Numbers Prove?

ON JANUARY 24, 2012, President Barack Obama said the following in his State of the Union Address:

> *"Right now—right now—American oil production is the highest that it's been in eight years. That's right—eight years. Not only that—last year, we relied less on foreign oil than in any of the past 16 years."*

The President was arguing that the U.S. *imported* less foreign oil because the U.S. *produced* more oil. Let's assume for a moment that the numbers were accurate; American oil production *increased*, and reliance on foreign oil *decreased*. What do these numbers mean? Do they really prove that reliance on foreign oil decreased *because* American oil production increased? Or, is it possible that reliance on foreign oil decreased because a weak U.S. economy decreased *demand* for oil?

Six days after the President's speech, Marketwatch.com reported that the cost of oil had been dropping, "after weaker-than-expected fourth-quarter U.S. economic growth also raised doubts about demand outlook." And that same day, Foxbusiness.com reported that U.S. oil demand dropped 1.3%, according to "revised government data released Monday." So even the government's own data indicated lower U.S. demand for oil!

Every February, the National Football League (NFL) invites the best college football players in the nation to its Scouting Combine, where NFL executives, coaches, scouts, and medical personnel from all thirty-two NFL teams evaluate the college players eligible for the upcoming NFL Draft. Athletes are measured for size, speed, and strength using tests such as the forty-yard dash, bench press, vertical jump, broad jump, twenty-yard shuttle, three-cone drill, and others. But what do these numbers prove? The ultimate question for NFL executives is whether the college player will do well in the NFL. Will the athlete's performance in college "translate" to the NFL? The Combine numbers do not necessarily answer this question.

JaMarcus Russell, from LSU, had a pretty good Combine in 2007, measuring in at 6 feet 5½ inches, 265 pounds, completing the forty-yard dash in 4.72 seconds (Tom Brady's time was 5.28 seconds in 2000), and a vertical leap of 31 inches (Brady's was 24.5 inches). ESPN reported that Russell's Combine workouts, arm strength, and size impressed several teams. The Oakland Raiders selected Russell with the first overall pick of the 2007 NFL Draft and signed him to a contract for $61 million, with $32 million guaranteed. Three seasons later the Raiders released Russell because of inconsistent play, his record 7–18. Conversely, linebacker Terrell Suggs didn't have a great Combine. His forty-yard dash time was 4.84, with 19 repetitions on the bench press, and vertical jump 33 inches, all below-average or average numbers. Yet he turned out to be a great NFL player. He was Associated Press Defensive Rookie of the Year in 2003, Associated Press Defensive Player of the Year in 2011, has been to several Pro Bowls, and he won a Super Bowl (XLVII) with the Baltimore Ravens.

John Chambers, CEO of Cisco Systems, once said on Fareed Zakaria GPS that President Clinton's information age created twenty-two million jobs. He was speaking to the ongoing question of whether the digital revolution has been good for jobs or not. Assuming that that twenty-two million is accurate, and leaving aside the question of how much those jobs pay, does that number prove that the digital revolution has caused a net gain in jobs? Not yet. Other numbers are also relevant. We need to know the other side of the balance sheet. How many jobs has the digital revolution displaced, over the same period of time, by allowing the outsourcing of research and development, data entry, customer support, accounting, legal services, health care, engineering, and computer programming?

—THE KEY—
Even if the numbers are accurate,
question what they really indicate.

Watch Out for "Average" Arguments

IF YOUR REAL estate agent recommends you sell your house for $200,000 because that's the "average" sale price for homes in the neighborhood, you'll want to know what "average" means. The same goes for when a politician declares what the "average" voter wants, when a scientist states what the "average" temperature is; and pretty much anytime someone uses the word "average" in an argument. What does "average" mean? There are three main possibilities.

Mean average is an average of a set of numbers. First add all the items to get a sum total. For example, here are four items: 2, 4, 6, 8. Add them up to get a sum of 20. Then divide the sum of 20 by the number of items (4) to get a mean average of 5. Quiz! What's the mean average of 2, 3, and 10? (Answer: 5.)

Median average is the middle number in a set of numbers. For example, here's a set of numbers: 2, 3, 10. The median average is 3, the middle number in the set. Quiz! What's the median average of 2, 3, 10, 20, and 50? (Answer: 10.)

No Clue average—sometimes the person using the word "average" has no clue what the average is. They're just throwing out a number and hoping you like it. It's an easy thing to say when you're desperate to make a point: "The average [blah, blah, blah]!"

So what does your real estate agent mean by "average"? Ask for neighborhood sale prices so you can do the math and calculate the mean and median averages. For example, neighborhood home sales of $198,000, $200,000, and $250,000 provide a mean average of $216,000 and a median of $200,000. The difference is $16,000, a significant amount. If you're selling, you'll argue the mean average is more fair and accurate, because you want a higher number. If you're buying, you'll argue the median.

I recently read a story on Money.cnn.com that Americans' mean average wealth was about $301,000 per adult. But Americans' median wealth was only about $44,900 per adult. The explanation for the difference was that the high number of very rich Americans skewed the mean average upwards.

—THE KEY—
Define what "average" means.

Is the Sample Big Enough?

STATISTICS OFTEN SEEK to learn something about a large group of things by examining a small sample of the group. For example, a public opinion poll may want to estimate the percentage of voters likely to vote for one presidential candidate over another. Rather than ask 200 million voters (the entire group or "population" of voters), the polling company might ask 1,000 (a small sample of voters). Asking 1,000 is not as accurate as asking all 200 million, of course, but that's how statistics work. "Sampling" is a relatively quick, cheap, and practical way to make predictions or estimates. So how many people should be polled? How large should the sample be? There are free calculators on the Internet that you can use to find out how large a sample should be. Just punch in:

    a. the size of the whole group (e.g., 200,000 voters);

    b. the margin of error that you can live with (e.g., plus or minus 4%); and

c. the confidence level you're aiming for (i.e., do you want to be 90%, 95%, or 99% reliable?).

For example, if the whole group (or "population") is 200,000 and you are okay with a margin of error of +/- 4%, and a confidence level of 95%, then the sample size should be about 599. If the whole group is 5,000 and you're aiming for a margin of error of +/- 4% and a confidence level of 95%, then the sample size should be about 537.

Let's say you want to buy a home. Your real estate agent says the average home sale during the last twelve months in your city is $150,000. The agent bases this number on three home sales. But it turns out that 100 homes were sold during the last twelve months. Using an Internet sample calculator, with a margin of error of +/- 4% and a confidence level of 95%, the sample needs to be eighty-six home sales! Yet your agent based his average on only three home sales! His estimate of $150,000 could be accurate, but the sample is so small that it could be way off. Don't pay $150,000 until your agent revises his estimate based on an adequate sample size.

Similarly, if someone tells you most American women don't want to marry, and they base this conclusion on talking with a half a dozen friends, this is not solid statistics. The sample is simply too small. So don't make a hasty generalization based on too few examples.

After the Deepwater Horizon oil spill in the Gulf of Mexico, the federal government banned all deepwater drilling for oil in the Gulf of Mexico. The next month, a federal court invalidated the ban on deepwater drilling. The Judge explained that in deciding to ban all deepwater drilling, the government focused on only one incident:

"Deepwater Horizon and BP [British Petroleum] only. None others." The government assumed that "because one rig failed and although no one yet fully knows why, all companies and rigs drilling new wells over 500 feet also universally present an imminent danger." The Judge summed up the error of hasty generalizations rather nicely: "If some drilling equipment parts are flawed, is it rational to say all are? Are all airplanes a danger because one was? All oil tankers like Exxon Valdez? All trains? All mines? That sort of thinking seems heavy handed, and rather overbearing."

—THE KEY—
Check sample size.

Is the Sample Relevant?

I HEARD A story on the radio about a gentleman who hitchhiked across the country. He explained that he never had a bad experience. As a result, his faith in humanity increased. He was encouraged about the kindness of people. Can you see the problem here? The gentleman based his opinion only on those people who were kind enough to give him a ride! What about all the drivers who passed him by? How kind were they? The "sample" of people included only persons nice enough to give him a ride, and was not a fair representation of all of humanity.

If you want to buy a two-bedroom condo in your city, you'll want to know the average sale price for two-bedroom condos in the area during the last twelve months. So you'll ask your real estate agent, who will review some statistics and get back to you. But if your agent includes sales of three-bedroom condos, the sample is not relevant because three-bedroom condos are generally more expensive than two-bedroom condos. And if your agent includes sales of detached homes, again the sample is not relevant because detached homes are also more expensive than condos. A relevant sample will include two-bedroom condos in the area, and that's it.

Public opinion polls must also be careful to contact a relevant sample group. For example, answers to many questions depend partly on factors such as gender, age, residence, race, and political party. Also, studies show that women answer the phone more than men, older people answer the phone more than younger people, and rural residents answer the phone more than urban residents. So if a public opinion poll does not consider these tendencies, the sample will be dominated by older, rural women, and the statistics might not accurately reflect the larger population as a whole.

The morning news often includes the result of a study, perhaps on health, the environment, or almost anything imaginable. The first thought of many is possible bias, so it's asked who did the study and who paid for it. But this is a little superficial, as a study could be accurate regardless who did it or paid for it. A more probing question is often about the sample. If it's a study on health, who were the test subjects? If it's a study on treatment, was there a control group (to provide a standard for comparison)? Was it a blind or double-blind study? (In a blind study the subjects don't know whether they are part of the test group or control group, and in a double-blind study the investigators don't know either.) In general, where did the data come from and does it accurately reflect a bigger picture?

—The Key—
Make sure the sample is relevant.

Don't Argue Faith

FAITH IS HOPE, trust, or belief that is not based on proof. You just believe it. The most common example is belief in God. Some offer proof that God exists, but ultimately it is a matter of faith. You may have faith in something when there is absolutely no evidence to support your belief. You may also have faith in something when there is overwhelming evidence that contradicts your belief! Faith can come from religious beliefs, upbringing, or personality traits such as optimism, determination, or perseverance. And it can be very powerful. (See the book *The Power of Positive Thinking* by Dr. Norman Vincent Peale.) But the key is, faith doesn't come from facts.

As faith is not based on evidence, and is not rational, it's not something you can argue about. After all, what is there to argue about? You either believe or you don't. You can't argue about facts, evidence, or reasoning, because faith is not based on these things. They're irrelevant to the issue of faith. So don't feel pressure to justify your faith. Nor should you try to undermine someone else's faith. Just acknowledge that it's a matter of faith and let it be. This also highlights the problem with interfaith disputes; they can never be resolved, and they usually just antagonize people. Nobody likes others to question their faith.

One last thought. Before taking the gloves off and calling something a matter of faith, make sure it really is a belief based on faith. For example, a person may believe something and call it a "matter of faith" as a way of avoiding argument. In reality, their belief is based on facts they believe to be true and reasoning they think is sound. And when their facts and reasoning are undermined, they give up their "faith."

—THE KEY—

Don't argue about something that is truly a matter of faith.

Original Sin

DON'T FALL FOR an argument that relies solely on the origin of something and ignores the current reality. How something started is not always relevant to what it is today. Easter may have started as a pagan spring festival, but does that undermine its legitimacy today? Easter is now celebrated by Christians as the resurrection of Jesus Christ and is typically the most well-attended service of the year. Australia was originally populated by aboriginal people—hunters and gatherers—and then settled by the British through the transportation of large numbers of male and female prisoners. So is Australia uncivilized? Hardly. Today Australia has one of the world's largest economies, and life expectancy in Australia is also among the highest in the world.

The reverse of an "original sin" argument might be called a "great start" argument. Here a person argues that because something had a great beginning, it's still great today. I've known people whose parents or grandparents were very wealthy, accomplished, or perhaps even members of a royal family. And so they think quite a bit of themselves and speak often about their distinguished heritage. While their family history may be interesting, it doesn't say anything about the individuals. People are not automatically exceptional just because their ancestors were. A close relative of this argument is "resting on laurels." Here a person did have some noteworthy accomplishment in the past and believes that it makes the person somehow exceptional now. These people tend to have strong memories and are fond of retelling their past glories. Companies sometimes do this too, marketing their brand based on successes of the past but failing to do anything exceptional today.

And therein lies the key. As any mutual fund prospectus will tell you, past performance does not necessarily predict future results. Consider current circumstances.

—THE KEY—
Don't get hung up on how something started;
consider the current reality.

A Cliché Is Not an Argument

CLICHÉS ARE GENERALIZATIONS based on centuries of living. And they're often true, in a *general* kind of way. But a cliché should not be used to argue for or against something in a *particular* case. Simply said, a cliché is not a substitute for an argument.

"Patience is a virtue." Sometimes it is. But if your 401(k) is losing money year after year, should you be patient and do nothing? If you have applied for a job and received no response, should you just sit back and be patient? Of course not. Sometimes patience can hurt you. Sometimes you need to take action.

"All publicity is good publicity." Maybe it is, if all you care about is notoriety. But if your company is publicly accused of ripping off customers, is that good? If you are publicly accused of being indecent, does that bode well for your future?

"Don't change horses in midstream." I've never ridden a horse, but this sounds like good advice. But does that mean that if your lawyer is routinely late to court and unprepared that you should stick with her? If you hired a contractor but he's using low-quality materials and his work is sloppy, should you just let him finish the job? Of course not! Sometimes it's better to make a change.

"Fight fire with fire." Professional firefighters do this sometimes. "Backburning" is a way of fighting a bushfire by burning back towards the oncoming fire, thereby removing fuel from the path of the fire. But if the person you are arguing with insults you, should you insult him or her? If the other person makes a "domino" argument, should you make one too? Of course not. It's a mistake to respond to a mistake by making a mistake.

"The end justifies the means." Here's a cliché that could end civilization! Would the United States be justified in ending its dependence on foreign oil by seizing a few Middle Eastern countries? Would a business be justified in increasing profit by charging for unneeded services? The end goal may be legitimate and worth pursuing, but the methods used to achieve the goal must be also be legitimate.

"A leopard cannot change its spots" and "you can't teach an old dog new tricks." I suppose a leopard can't change its spots. And I'll let a dog expert handle the dog cliché. But if you have an anger management problem that interferes with your daily life, should you simply ignore it? If you're having a hard time learning a new skill, should you just quit? If you are very experienced in your industry but you have become aware that there is a better way to do something, should you ignore it? Aristotle said the main difference between people and rocks is that people *can* change their behavior. Rocks can't. Throw a rock in the air and it's going to fall back to the ground, every time, no matter how much you want it to stay in the air. But if you want to be more courageous, just act more courageous. Practice it. Fake it, if you have to. Make it a habit. Eventually, you'll become more courageous. The same goes for acquiring other virtues. You're not a rock.

Clichés and other sayings are cute and catchy. But they're not arguments. So be careful how you use them, or how people use them on you.

—The Key—
Don't argue by cliché.

Lack of Proof

IF YOU CAN'T find your keys, and you search your entire car, and you don't find your keys in your car, it's okay to say your keys are not in your car. You are making an argument (*keys aren't in car*) based on lack of evidence (*didn't find keys in car*). This argument is valid because you searched the *entire* car. So the lack of proof that your keys are in your car proves your keys are not in your car.

If you argue extraterrestrials do not exist because you have never seen evidence of extraterrestrials, you are also making an argument (*extraterrestrials don't exist*) based on lack of evidence (*haven't seen evidence of extraterrestrials*). But this argument is not as strong, because you have not searched the entire universe for evidence of aliens. In fact, when you think about how big the universe is, you probably have not even searched a significant portion of the universe. So the lack of proof of extraterrestrials does not necessarily prove that extraterrestrials don't exist. Maybe they do exist; *you just haven't looked in the right places!*

So you can make a valid argument that something is not true, or does not exist, based on lack of proof, if you have explored all possible sources of proof. But if you have not explored all possible sources of proof, then your argument is speculative and not as strong.

Earlier I discussed the idea that some arguments have a conclusion that provides *certainty*, while other arguments have a conclusion that provides only a *probability*. Consider that idea here. For example, if you can't find your keys, and you search 75% of your home, and you don't find your keys in your home, you cannot say with certainty that your keys are not in your home, because you haven't searched your entire home. But you searched most of it. So you can say that your keys are probably not in your home. But if you search only 25% of your home and did not find your keys, you cannot say that your keys are probably not in your home. You have not searched enough of your home to say that.

—The Key—
Consider carefully what lack of proof really proves.

A Threat Is Not an Argument

THE U.S. ARMY Field Manual gives instructions for interrogating prisoners of war and unlawful combatants. One of the techniques is "fear-up." Basically, the interrogator makes the prisoner fear that he may be killed if he cooperates, unless he gets protection. The interrogator may say, for example, "Do you know what can happen to you here?" Salespersons sometimes use this technique, though more subtly. If you don't buy the extended warranty, protective coating, stain protection, antivirus program ("that we sell"), special electric toothbrush, face cream, or ACH Direct-Debit payment from your checking account, "then you'll regret it." Without any additional facts or reasons to support the claim, this is a threat, not an argument.

Another interrogation technique from the Field Manual is "fear-down." Here the interrogator reassures the other person by acting as his or her "protector." Salespersons also use this technique sometimes. I had just landed at an airport in a country I had never visited and did not know very well. As soon as I stepped outside the airport with my bags and started looking for a taxi, a man approached me. He explained that many of the "taxis" were not properly licensed, that the drivers were not good, and that they overcharged. But he said he would "take care of me." So I went with him. Later I learned that the other taxis were properly licensed, that their fees are regulated and determined by meters, and that my "protector" charged me double the going rate.

During the 2004 United States presidential election, Vice President Dick Cheney told supporters this at a town-hall meeting:

> *"It's absolutely essential that eight weeks from today, on November 2, we make the right choice, because if we make the wrong choice then the danger is that we'll get hit again and we'll be hit in a way that will be devastating from the standpoint of the United States."*

Vice President Cheney was arguing that Americans should vote to reelect President George W. Bush or risk another terrorist attack. He was trying to persuade by fear.

"If you don't have disability insurance, your family could be one accident away from financial catastrophe." "If you don't hire my cousin, I don't know how much business I can send your way." These aren't arguments to insure against a disabling accident or hire a particular person. They're threats. They're statements intended to persuade by fear. A sound argument is based on facts and logic, not fear. So don't make an argument based on fear. And don't be persuaded by an argument based on fear.

—THE KEY—
A threat is not an argument.

Moderation Is Not Always Best

MODERATION IS AN ancient virtue. And moderation can be beneficial at times—for example, in diet, exercise, rest, and work. But moderation is not always the best solution to a problem. Compromise is not always the best outcome for a dispute. If you want your child to finish his or her homework, but your child doesn't want to, should you compromise and let your child finish only half of the homework? Is it okay to tell the truth only half the time? If you're in charge of information technology in your company, should you install antivirus software on only half of the company's computers?

You've heard the expression, "It's the principle of the thing." It's often uttered by someone who is being completely bullheaded about something and refuses to budge. They just flat out refuse to compromise. Not even an inch. Well, sometimes they're right. Sometimes the principle is so important that moderation or compromise is not a solution—it's failure. The trick is recognizing when moderation or compromise is okay, and when it's not. Here are some guidelines.

Moderation or compromise is fine when an extreme position is harmful and should be avoided. For example, eating too much of a particular food, not eating enough, not exercising at all, exercising too much, sleeping too much, and not sleeping enough can be harmful. Compromise is also good when the arguments are not sure things or "slam dunks" for either side. One side might have a better argument than the other, but both sides may have a fighting chance of being right. Many civil lawsuits fall into this category. Maybe it's not all that clear that the defendant did anything wrong, or that the plaintiff is injured as bad as he claims. These are good cases for compromise, because it's not 100% clear who's right. Sometimes there is a range of choices that is reasonable, so no particular position is exactly "right," to the exclusion of all other positions. Management is considering how much of a raise to give an hourly employee, fifty cents or a dollar an hour. Can one say that fifty cents is "right" and a dollar is "wrong"? Probably not. So if management is split on the issue, compromise is a reasonable solution.

Moderation or compromise should be avoided, however, if even the slightest compromise can lead to disaster. Internet security, airport security, and national security are a few examples. Nor is moderation or compromise a good idea when it comes to virtues. One of the nice things about human beings is that we have virtues. Virtues may come from religion, philosophy, a role model, or other sources. We don't always live up to them, but at least we have them. We have something to aim for. Something to strive for. But the moment a person compromises a virtue, he becomes a little less than what he can be. Perhaps one of the most famous statements against moderation is "Give me liberty, or give me death!," attributed to Patrick Henry in a speech to the Virginia Convention on March 23, 1775. And long before that, Epictetus (A.D. 50-130) said, "As you aim for such great goals [as being free and unhindered], remember that you must not undertake them by acting moderately."

—THE KEY—

Consider when moderation is good and when it's not.

Answer the Question!

IF YOU ASK a relevant question, you deserve a relevant answer. But you won't always get one. Often other people don't *want* to answer your question directly. Or maybe they don't *know* the answer. Or maybe they don't want to admit something that hurts their argument. But they still might give you an answer, perhaps a very long answer. And it may be an impressive sounding answer, spoken with great sincerity and passion (politicians?). It just won't answer your question.

David Duke ran for governor of Louisiana in 1991, and then he ran into Tim Russert. Russert hosted NBC's *Meet the Press* for many years and he was the best at asking follow-up questions, especially when the guest did not answer the question. Russert asked Duke which manufacturers were the three biggest employers in the state of Louisiana. Duke's answer was "Well, we have a number of employers in our state." Duke did not answer Russert's question. So Russert repeated the question, and to his credit Duke admitted, "I couldn't give you their names right off, Sir."

Sometimes a person will avoid answering a question by claiming they don't know the answer, when they do. Others may ask you to clarify your question, when they don't really need clarification. Sometimes you won't even notice that the other person didn't answer your question. They're just so articulate, charming, or whatever—you might even forget your question!

When a courtroom lawyer hears an answer that is not really an answer, she says, "Objection, non-responsive!" So listen carefully, and make sure you get an answer to your question.

—The Key—

Make sure to get a relevant answer to your question.

Look at Me!

IMAGINE SOMEONE is trying to convince you to exercise more. And the person says, "Look at me! I exercise every day, whether I feel like it or not!" You will probably say something like, "Good for you! Now leave me alone!" Maybe you are trying to persuade your child to do his or her homework. So you say, "Your sister *always* does her homework. In fact, she usually doesn't even *have* homework because she gets so much done at school!" Your child will probably not appreciate the comparison, and your words will have the opposite effect you're aiming for.

There are two reasons these comparisons don't work. First, they are not relevant. Why should anyone care how disciplined *you* are about exercise? Why would that encourage anyone to exercise more? Wouldn't someone rather know how *they* will benefit from more exercise? Similarly, why should your son care how wonderfully his sister completes her homework? Why would that make him want to do his? Wouldn't your son be more interested in how *he* would benefit from doing his homework, or suffer by not doing it? Say things that matter and you have a much better chance of success.

The second reason that "Look at me!" and "Look at her!" comparisons don't persuade is that they are annoying as hell! Who likes to be put down? You may have an important argument to make, with relevant points to explain, and the other person may be open-minded and ready to agree. But if you needle them with a "Look at me!" comparison, they're likely to disagree, just to annoy you!

—THE KEY—

Don't compare someone unfavorably to someone else.

Don't Appeal to Envy

COWORKER LISA SAYS you should not help coworker Susan because Susan makes a lot more money than you do. And Susan hasn't worked for the company half as long as you have. So why should you help her? Lisa is trying to persuade you based on envy. It's a weak argument because it's not based on facts and reason. Instead, it's based entirely on emotions, and not particularly admirable emotions at that. Decisions based on such crude emotions will not produce the best outcomes. They will produce only more troubling emotions. Lisa should focus her argument on things that matter. Is it your job to help Susan? Will Susan return the favor someday and help you? Will helping Susan help or hurt you somehow? Will helping Susan help or hurt the company somehow?

Politicians sometimes argue for raising taxes on the wealthy so that they will pay their "fair share." But if the only reason given for raising taxes on the wealthy is to make them pay their "fair share," the argument may be based on envy, in this case envy of the wealthy.

Winston Churchill alluded to this when he said "Socialism is a philosophy of failure, the creed of ignorance, and the gospel of envy." Raising taxes on the wealthy might be good policy in certain circumstances, but the argument should be based on facts and reasons, not merely an emotion.

—THE KEY—

Don't make a decision based on envy.

Don't Overuse "Racist"

ON JULY 31, 2012, the *International Herald Tribune* had a front page article titled "In Mideast, Romney Remarks Offend." While speaking in Jerusalem, Republican presidential candidate Mitt Romney compared high incomes in Israel with low incomes in the Palestinian areas. Based on his reading of *The Wealth and Poverty of Nations* by David S. Landes, Romney concluded that culture played a role in the different income levels of Israelis and Palestinians. A senior aide to President Mahmoud Abbas of the Palestinian Authority replied that Romney's opinion "is a racist statement and this man doesn't realize that the Palestinian economy cannot reach its potential because there is an Israeli occupation." The aide added, "It seems to me this man lacks information, knowledge, vision and understanding of this region and its people."

Racism is one of the worst beliefs that humans can have. Race-based prejudice, violence, and oppression have motivated genocide such as the holocaust, and slavery as practiced in the United States during the nineteenth century. So one should be careful before describing a statement as racist. Perhaps Romney was simply trying to explain why Israelis were prospering while Palestinians were not, and offer a possible explanation—culture. Maybe Romney was wrong, but was his statement really based on racial prejudice, dislike, or oppression? Had the aide not distracted the argument with such an inflammatory word as "racist," he could have provided more of the information, knowledge, and understanding of the region that he claimed Romney lacked. He could have explained more fully why Palestinians make so much less money than Israelis. He could have provided a stronger argument—an argument that could lead to improved conditions for the Palestinians.

A white police officer shoots a black person. Some immediately claim that the officer shot the person because of race. But the reason why the officer used deadly force may depend on several factors, such as training, risk to life or health of the officer or the public, adverse weather, night operations, physical fitness, or equipment, none of which involve race. Race could have motivated the shooting, but all possible relevant factors should be considered before calling the shooting racist.

—THE KEY—
Better to make a thorough argument than
simply say something is racist.

Attack Arguments, Not People

MAYBE YOU DON'T like the person you are arguing with. Maybe you never liked them. Or maybe you suddenly stopped liking them when they disagreed with you. Either way, it can be very tempting sometimes to attack the person instead of their argument.

Insulting the person is common. "You're just *ignorant*. That's why you disagree with me." "You don't like affirmative action because you're a *racist*."

Attacking a person's history or motives is also common. "You want less taxes because you're a *Republican*!" "You want less regulation because you work on *Wall Street*!" "You're against abortion because you're a *man*!" "You want corporations to pay more taxes, but *you* cheat on your own taxes." You say you're for clean energy, but you drive an *SUV*!" The medical community recommends immunizations only so pharmaceutical companies can make more *money*!

It may feel good to say these things, but they are usually irrelevant and inflammatory. So it's really important to understand the distinction between the person and the argument.

Bill Bennett was Secretary of Education from 1985 to 1988. In 1993 he edited an anthology on moral education titled *The Book of Virtues: A Treasury of Great Moral Stories*. In 2003 he admitted to excessive gambling and vowed to stop. The temptation is to say that his book has less merit because of his excessive gambling. The truth is that Bennett's gambling has nothing to do with the book. The book promotes certain virtues, for example, responsibility, honesty, and courage. If one questions whether these are virtues, or whether they are worth practicing, then one should examine whether Bennett makes a strong argument for the virtues in the book. Does he explain why these virtues are important? Does he explain what good comes from these virtues, or what harm comes in their absence? Does he give relevant examples from history? These questions are relevant because they will show how strong or weak Bennett's arguments for virtue are. But learning more about Bennett's personal life won't help at all. No offense intended, but Bennett, himself, is irrelevant! He could be a complete scumbag, but if he makes a strong argument for virtues, then it's a strong argument for virtues.

Pauline Phillips started an advice column called Dear Abby in 1956. Around the same time, Pauline's twin sister, Esther Lederer, started a similar column called Ann Landers. This caused a little friction between the two and they were estranged for some time. *Life Magazine* once described their relationship as the "most feverish female feud since Elizabeth sent Mary Queen of Scots to the chopping block." One may be tempted to discount the value of the advice the sisters gave in their columns because they could not even get along with each other. But that would be a mistake. The advice in Dear Abby and Ann Landers stands, or falls, on its own merits. Was the advice reasonable? Was the advice based on sound values such as honesty, responsibility, and respect? Did the advice help? These are relevant questions to ask if one wants to assess the value of the advice given. But it won't help any to know how often Pauline called Esther on the phone, or how many Thanksgiving dinners they shared. That's between them.

A celibate, unmarried Catholic priest gives marriage advice. The temptation is to ask, "What does he know about marriage?" But again, the advice should be assessed on its own merits, regardless of who gives it. Does the priest listen to the couple carefully to determine what the issues are? Is the advice reasonable, fair to both spouses, and based on sound values? These questions reveal how sound the advice is. But one learns nothing about the quality of the advice by asking whether the priest is married or has ever had sex.

Attacking the person instead of the argument is an old trick, going back at least to 441 BCE, when Sophocles wrote the play *Antigone*. In *Antigone*, young Haemon tries to persuade his father, Creon, to spare Antigone's life.

> CREON: *So, men our age, we're to be lectured, are we?— schooled by a boy his age?*
>
> HAEMON: *Only in what is right. But if I seem young, look less to my years and more to what I do.*

Creon attacks Haemon rather than Haemon's argument, and says essentially that Haemon is too young to know what's right. But

Haemon wisely sets his father straight.

The list of similar examples is endless. Should a person suffering from depression seek treatment only from a therapist who has also suffered from depression? Should women seek treatment only from female OB/GYNs because male OB/GYNs have never been pregnant or had a menstrual period?

The only time a person's character, history, or motives are relevant is when credibility is at stake. For example, let's say you are requesting bids on a project. One contractor submits a bid with the earliest completion date and smallest budget. In this case, his credibility is relevant. He claims he can finish by a certain time for a certain cost; relevant proof would be his prior work history. If his last three projects were late and over budget, you might not want to accept his bid based on his promises for time and budget.

If a candidate is running for election and arguing her excellent character is one of the reasons why she should be elected, then her character is at issue. Her personal history is fair game for argument. Does she have a history for being honest, hard-working, and loyal? Or does her history reveal corruption, neglect, or double-crossing? An effective way to assess character is to look at prior acts.

But if credibility is not an issue, then a person's character, history, and motives are irrelevant. So if you are tempted to attack the person, turn your thoughts back to your argument. If the person is not aware of important facts, don't insult their ignorance—explain the facts to them. If the other person seems biased because of their occupation or beliefs, don't just accuse them of bias—explain the reasons why you think your argument is stronger. Focus on the point you want to make, and the reasons or facts that support your point.

116

Someone might attack *you* instead of your argument. If your credibility is an issue, then your character, history, and motives are fair game. But if your credibility is not an issue, don't fight fire with fire. Resist the temptation to counterattack the other person. Instead, focus the other person's attention back onto the argument.

—The Key—

When tempted to attack the person, attack the argument instead.

Appeal to Arguments, Not People

THIS ONE'S A "CHARMER." Sometimes you'll hear someone *appeal* to, rather than attack, a person's characteristics. "As a *Democrat,* you should be in favor of extending unemployment benefits." "As a *Christian,* you would of course be against the death penalty." "As a *victim* of a public mass shooting, I expect you would be in favor of an assault weapons ban." "Real *Americans* will support my candidacy."

Should all Democrats favor extending unemployment benefits just because they're Democrats? Should all Christians oppose the death penalty because they're Christians? Of course not. The real issues in these two arguments are *why* unemployment benefits should be extended, or *why* the death penalty should be abolished. Are all crime victims necessarily experts on public policy issues concerning gun control, or criminal sentencing? No, they're not.

Appealing to a person's characteristics is not an argument. It's a solicitation, like asking for money. That's fine, if all you want to do is solicit an opinion. But if you want to make a strong argument that can withstand attack, make an argument. Make a point and support it with reasons.

—THE KEY—

Use facts and reason, rather than charm and circumstance, to persuade.

Uncover Assumptions

IMAGINE TWO PEOPLE getting ready to arm wrestle. They sit down. They put their elbows on the table. And the moment they clasp hands one person suddenly starts the match, slams the other person's arm to the table, and "wins" the match.

Sneaking assumptions into arguments is similar, an unfair fast start. A famous and rather blatant example is, "Have you stopped beating your wife?" If the person says "Yes," he seems to admit he beat his wife in the past. If the person says "No," he seems to admit he is beating his wife now. The problem is that the question assumes the person started beating his wife at some point.

A car salesperson says to the buyer, "You can afford this car—you're a lawyer!" The argument assumes the lawyer's income is greater than the lawyer's expenses, and that the extra income is enough to buy the car.

In court, a lawyer would object to these statements and say, "Assumes facts not in evidence!" The statements assume certain facts to be true that have not yet been proven.

Some assumptions are hard to spot. For example, some argue that homosexuality and gay marriage are immoral because they are "unnatural." Others argue that certain food, medicine, or even clothing is better if it is all "natural." These arguments assume, without any discussion, that what is natural is *always* better and what is unnatural is *always* worse. But that's not always true. Natural disasters and disease are "natural," and generally considered undesirable.

So your first task is to uncover the assumption. Dig it out and understand what it is. If you don't notice the assumption, you can't ask if it's true or not. That might leave the argument with a major flaw or weakness.

Second, ask if the assumption is true. You can quickly and easily show that certain assumptions are true or false, for example, whether the lawyer really has enough money left, after expenses, to afford a car. But other assumptions need to be discussed at length. They become arguments unto themselves! For example, is "natural" always better?

Hypothetical questions are a different matter. It's okay to assume, for the purpose of a hypothetical question, that a fact is true. For example, "Assuming the car was travelling 40 miles an hour, the road was dry, and the tires were in good condition and properly inflated, how much distance would it take the car to stop?" Hypothetical questions like this are okay because the assumptions are out in the open and not hidden.

—The Key—

Uncover "hidden" assumptions and make sure they are true.

Don't Be Led by "Leading" Questions

SOMETIMES A PERSON will try to lead you to say something by the way they phrase a question. For example, "You're not *really* going to join the military, are you? You don't *really* believe that he loves you, do you? These questions "lead" you to the desired answer because of the way they are phrased. Even the person's tone and the way they ask the question are designed to make you feel stupid if you disagree. Well, don't feel stupid! And don't be "led" to believe anything. Ask *why* you should believe.

Why shouldn't I join the military? Give me reasons. Analyze the potential risks and rewards, both what I might give up by joining the military (opportunity cost) and what I might gain. Why don't you think he loves me? What do you know about what he does for me, how he cares for me, and the nature of our relationship?

—THE KEY—

Don't let the tone or phrasing of a question "lead" you to an answer.

Be Tone Deaf

I'VE SEEN SOME SPEAKERS who are so dull that they actually take my breath away. My breathing becomes shallow and I have shortness of breath. Their voices are monotonous, never changing in volume or tone. Their facial expression never changes. Legal seminars are a great place to find such speakers. Occasionally you'll encounter dull speakers on the radio or TV.

Other speakers act like they are giving an Academy Award performance. Their voices range from soft, quiet lows to thunderous, climactic highs. They raise their eyebrows, drop their jaws, gesture with their hands and sometimes their entire body.

It's tempting to dismiss the dull speaker as unpersuasive, or agree with the more animated speaker. But try pushing the mute button on your TV and reading the closed captions. You may find that the dull speaker makes very clear points and supports them with relevant facts or reasons. And maybe the more exciting speaker is just saying bland, simplistic stuff, not making any points or backing them up with reasons—he just looks great doing it!

Sometimes when a person wants you to be lenient, they will lower their voice, almost to a whisper. It's their way of pleading with you. But should the volume of their voice affect your decision to be lenient?

Another person may want you to take harsh action, like punish someone. So they raise their voice, like they're leading a battlefield charge. But again, do you want to be persuaded by the volume of a person's voice?

—THE KEY—

Don't be persuaded by a person's tone; focus on their argument.

Sincerely,

A SALESPERSON TAKES a deep breath and exhales audibly. She pauses noticeably. She leans forward, puts a hand on your shoulder, looks you in the eye, and with all the sincerity she can muster says, "You look *fantastic* in that suit."

Sincerity, whether real or feigned, can get your attention. The other person hopes that you will agree with them when you realize how sincere they are, how much they believe they are right, and how much they care about you. Salespeople often use sincerity to build rapport and make a sale easier. Suddenly everything about you is interesting, wonderfully unique, and impossible to fault. You are just *perfect*! How about that! The U.S. Army Field Manual (which describes techniques for interrogating prisoners of war) includes a technique called "ego-up." The interrogator flatters and compliments the other person, sometimes with a sense of awe, to build up their ego and persuade them to give information.

Sincerity is moving, and flattery feels good. But if you make a decision solely because someone boosted your ego, you may make a mistake. I was shopping for a suit once and all of a sudden I had a perfect body: waist, shoulders, everything. I was beginning to wonder how I ended up a lawyer instead of a model. Anyway, I bought the suit, the most expensive one ever for me. And then over the next three weeks, I proceeded to have both the pants and the jacket altered three times because it was not only the most expensive suit I had ever bought, it was the worst-fitting. I decided never to buy another suit from this particular salesperson, who happened to be very experienced. Unfortunately it seems her experience was focused more on flattery than fit.

Sometimes you need to know if you can trust someone. For example, maybe you need a website. A website developer shows you samples of websites he has created. They look great. He quotes you a price. It seems fair. But you know he's a busy guy. His phone keeps ringing, even while you are talking with him. And he postponed this meeting with you, twice. Everything else seems okay, but you are starting to wonder if this guy can finish the job on time. You need to know if you can trust him. You tell him that. And he gives you the sincere treatment—the deep breath, the pause, the eye contact—and says, "*Trust me*, I will get this job done for you, on time, *guaranteed.*"

Is that enough? Maybe he's being truthful, but how do you know? What else is he going to say? "I'm swamped and probably won't get it done on time but I really need the money"? If he says that, he'll lose the job, and he knows it. If you accept his argument based only on his sincerity, you risk getting burned. You need something else. This is a case where personal credibility is an issue. Put his sincerity aside for a moment and get more information on his history. Call the last two companies he built websites for and ask if the websites were finished on time. Get some facts and don't rely solely on sincerity.

—THE KEY—
Rely on facts, not flattery or sincerity.

Don't Nauseate People

SOMETIMES PEOPLE TRY to persuade by repeating a claim over and over. They don't give any facts or reasons to support their claim, so it's not really a full-fledged argument. It's just a claim, and they say it over and over ("ad nauseam," or to the point of nausea). "I keep telling you, you need to buy a house!" "I must have told you a thousand times that you should study computer programming."

I recently heard two guys on the radio arguing about a famous athlete who was charged with murder. One argued that people should not assume the athlete was guilty; he recited the well-known maxim that people are presumed innocent until proven guilty. The other fellow just kept repeating, "But he's accused of *murder!*" And every time he said it, he would emphasize the word "murder" even more. Repeating a claim—without giving any reasons to believe it—doesn't make it stronger. It just makes it more annoying.

Groups of people repeat claims too. You may hear a point repeated by different sources over a period of time, for example, that certain ethnicities have certain traits or characteristics. It might not be true, and the claim may lack reliable factual support. But if it's repeated enough times, it can lead to stereotyping and even racism. Eventually, people stop analyzing whether it's true; they just accept it as fact, even if it's not.

—THE KEY—

Repeating a claim over and over doesn't make it true.

Don't Jump on the Bandwagon

THE LATEST "BLOCKBUSTER" movie has lines around the block. Does that mean it's a great movie? A restaurant is so busy that you can't get a table unless you make a reservation three months in advance. Does that prove the restaurant's food and service are the best in town? A new book is a "#1 bestseller." Does that prove it's the best book on the market?

There may be many reasons why a movie, restaurant, or book is popular. And the reasons might have nothing to do with quality, merit, or truth. So relying on public opinion is not always the most reliable way to judge something. Sometimes you really can't tell unless you try it, and judge for yourself.

A recent poll showed that 62% of Americans think the government should cut spending to help the economy. So is that all we need to know? Just start cutting? Whether spending cuts ("austerity measures") will help or hurt the economy depends on many factors, for example, the effects on the poor and middle class, government's ability to pay its debt liabilities, investors' trust in a government's ability to pay its debts, effects on interest rates, and even psychological factors. It's more complicated than a public opinion poll.

And public opinion changes. Another recent poll showed that 87% of Americans favor marriage between blacks and whites. In 1958 it was 4%.

Public opinion does have a certain allure. It can feel a little uncomfortable to hold a minority viewpoint. Politicians play on this emotion by arguing, "most people agree that . . ." or "most people don't support . . ." But sometimes the minority is right!

Also, public opinion polls can seem authoritative because they involve statistics and numbers. But remember what your parents used to say: "If all your friends jump off a cliff, are you going to jump too?" Just because a lot of people believe something, or are doing something, doesn't prove it's a good idea.

—THE KEY—
Don't jump on the bandwagon
just because a lot of other people are.

Don't Assume Generalizations Are Always True

LIFE WITHOUT GENERALIZATIONS would be pretty scary. For example, people generally believe that killing other people is wrong. And thank goodness they do! Imagine if they didn't! But generalizations have exceptions. If a suicide bomber is about to detonate explosives in an outdoor food market full of shoppers, would you want law enforcement to follow the generalization (that killing is wrong) and not do anything? You would probably prefer that law enforcement intervene and kill the terrorist if necessary to save the lives of others.

People generally believe lying is wrong. But if your daughter's ex-boyfriend comes up to your front door holding a gun, smelling of alcohol, and asking if your daughter is home because he "just wants to talk with her," would you say yes?

So generalizations apply "generally," but not in every single case. Sometimes, the situation calls for an exception to the general rule. Assuming that generalizations are always true, without exception, is a mistake. So be wary of statements that include words like *always, never, all, none, everyone,* or *nobody.*

In divorce, it's generally true that the wife needs spousal support more than the husband. Alabama once had a law that required husbands to pay alimony, but not wives. Wives could not be ordered to pay alimony under the law. In *Orr v. Orr,* the U.S. Supreme Court struck down the law. The Court explained that some families "defied the stereotype," and left the husband dependent on the wife. So the Court said that hearings should be required in each case to see who needs the support, the wife or the husband.

So when you encounter an exceptional case or situation, does that mean that the generalization is false? It depends. If one generalizes that *all* African Americans are Democrats, and there is at least one African American who is a Republican, then the generalization is false. But if one says that African Americans are *generally* Democrats, then the existence of a several Republican African Americans does not make the generalization false. If most African Americans are Democrats, the generalization would still be true. Just determine whether the generalization is phrased in a way that allows for any exceptions. For example, "Americans *generally* pay their taxes" is a generalization that allows for some exceptions. "*Everyone* in America pays their taxes" does not allow for exceptions.

—THE KEY—

Don't assume that generalizations apply in every single case.

The Difference Between
"Sufficient" and "Necessary"

CAUSATION IS THE idea that one thing causes another. A common issue is whether something is "sufficient," all by itself, to cause another thing; or whether it's just one of several things that are "necessary" to cause another thing.

Rain, for example, is "sufficient" to make the ground wet. You don't need anything else to happen. If it rains, the ground will be wet.

Clouds, on the other hand, are "necessary" to make the ground wet, because you can't have rain without clouds. But clouds alone are not "sufficient" to make the ground wet. You can have clouds without rain, and the ground will be dry.

Let's say you start a business. You want your business to succeed. You may think that if your business idea is good enough, your business will succeed. You might believe, in other words, that your great business idea is "sufficient" to make your business a success. But in reality your business idea is probably not "sufficient" to cause success. Most successful businesses require a lot of hard work, persistence, marketing, and even some luck. Your business idea may be "necessary" for success, but it's probably not "sufficient," all by itself, to cause success. You need some other things to happen too.

Now you're ready to attack this familiar saying: "Practice makes perfect." What's the flaw in that statement? The saying assumes that practice, alone, will cause you to become perfect at something—that practice is "sufficient" to cause perfection. But all the practice in the world won't make you perfect if you're practicing the wrong way and following bad habits. And if you are not well-suited for the activity, even the best practice habits won't make you perfect. You can take singing lessons from the best instructors in the world, but if you are tone deaf, you still won't sing well. So practice is "necessary" to become "perfect," because one cannot improve without it. But it's not "sufficient" to be perfect. Other things are needed too, for example, practicing good habits and being well-suited for the activity.

—THE KEY—

Distinguish what is "sufficient" from what is "necessary."

Don't Confuse Cause and Effect

SOME ARGUE THAT violent video games, movies, television shows, and music cause anger, aggression, and violent behavior. Violent media is the cause, and violent society is the effect.

But others argue that society has always been violent, and that violent media simply mirrors society. Art imitates life. Shakespeare's Macbeth was beheaded long before violent video games.

Regarding violence in media and society, it may not be clear what is cause and what is effect. Maybe another factor is causing both increased violence in media and society. Further study is needed. In the meantime, neither side should simply assume without analysis that one thing causes another.

Katrina's employer gives her a pay raise, making her the highest paid employee in the company. Katrina's coworkers complain that the employer is favoring Katrina. "Obviously she makes the most money. The company treats her special."

Analyze the coworkers' argument. Can you see a possible flaw?

Think about cause and effect. The coworkers argue that the company's treatment of Katrina caused her to make the most money. But is the company's treatment of Katrina a cause, or an effect? What if Katrina is always on time, helps other employees, is very productive and accurate, and never complains. Maybe *that's* why the company made her the highest paid employee. Katrina's excellent work caused her high pay and special treatment.

Or it could be both. Maybe Katrina is an excellent worker, causing her employer to make her the highest paid employee; and her high salary encourages her and causes her to work even harder! It's a vicious cycle of work and pay!

Jacob is a positive thinker—always optimistic and never in a bad mood, this fellow. He also has a great career, marriage, and pretty much anything a guy can ask for. "Of course he's a positive thinker. His life is perfect!"

Attack! What's wrong with that statement? The claim is that Jacob's perfect life causes him to be a positive thinker. But could it be that Jacob's positive attitude causes his life to be better?

—THE KEY—

Don't assume, without any analysis, that one thing causes another.

Don't Confuse Timing with Cause

YOU BORROW A friend's car and the engine starts making a loud knocking noise and emitting thick smoke from the tailpipe. Your friend blames you. Your friend assumes that because his car broke down *after* he loaned it to you, you must have caused his car to break down. Of course, it may just be coincidence. Maybe the car was ready to break down, no matter who drove it. Or maybe you did break it! The point is that timing does not always prove cause.

You're not feeling well, so you take a special remedy a friend recommended. Then you start feeling better. Did the remedy work? Maybe it did. Then again, maybe your illness just needed a little time to go away, whether you got treatment or not.

A state passes a strict gun control law. Then gun violence decreases in that state. Did the law reduce gun violence? You know to look beyond the timing of events. What else would you want to know to make a sound conclusion? Did all violent crime (not just gun violence) decrease in the state? If all violent crime decreased, then maybe something else caused both violent crime and gun violence to decrease. What about gun violence in other states with more liberal gun control laws? Did gun violence decrease in those states too? If so, there might be some other factor that is decreasing gun violence nationwide. These are just a few facts you need to know, beyond the mere timing of the law, to reach a sound conclusion.

A child receives various vaccines (chickenpox, hepatitis, measles, polio, etc.). Later, the child is diagnosed with a serious health problem. Can one say that the vaccine probably caused the illness simply because the illness happened after the vaccine? No, the timing alone is not enough information to make this conclusion. The Centers for Disease Control and Prevention (CDC) recently addressed this issue on their website. Some people believed that a certain vaccine caused sudden infant death syndrome (SIDS) because in some cases SIDS occurred a few days after the shot. But the CDC explained that controlled studies showed that SIDS always occurred at the age when babies get their routine shots, whether they get the shots or not.

When timing is confused with cause, superstition sometimes follows. "A black cat crossed the road up ahead and now my car is acting up." Did the black cat really cause the car to malfunction, or was it just a coincidence of timing? "I spilled some salt and now I have an upset stomach." Did salt falling to the ground really cause gastrointestinal problems? One nice thing about superstitious beliefs is that they show humility. Lots of things can happen in life that we have no control over. Superstitions at least show that people don't think too much of themselves and that they have some respect for circumstances beyond their control. But sound reasoning requires more than timing to prove causation. Just because one thing follows another doesn't mean the first thing caused the second. Sometimes things happen coincidentally, for better or worse—hopefully for better!

—The Key—
Don't assume, without any analysis, that one thing
caused another thing just because of the timing of events.

Make Strong Analogies

PROFESSOR CRONQUIST, ONE of my philosophy professors, once said that intelligence is the ability to make connections and distinctions—to understand that two things are related in some way, or unrelated.

Arguing by analogy is a *fantastic* way to make a point, and it's basically making a connection between what you're trying to prove and something else. But the analogy must be strong. So what's a strong analogy?

First, a strong analogy has several important similarities. For example, you might say that maintaining your health is like maintaining a car. If you put high quality fuel and fluids in your car, drive your car on a regular basis, take your car to a good mechanic for regular service, and don't abuse it, your car will perform better and last longer. Similarly, if you eat healthy food, exercise on a regular basis, visit a good doctor for regular checkups, and don't abuse yourself, you will be healthier and live longer. This analogy is strong because it shows several important similarities between what you're trying to prove and something else. It makes a connection, and shows how two different things are related in some way.

But the similarities must also be relevant. If they're not, then the analogy is weak. For example, one might argue that relationships are like investments. You get out of them what you put into them, right? And with investments, it's important not to "put all your eggs in one basket." You should *diversify* your investments and spread them around. That way if any one investment loses money, your entire portfolio of investments won't lose money. Can you see the analogy coming? Your spouse or committed partner says that your relationship is "*just like an investment*." So, the two of you should be free to date other people, to "*diversify*" your relationships. How does that sound? Not so committed, it seems.

Relationships are like investments in that the more you invest (money in the case of investments, time and attention in the case of relationships), the more you get out of them. But while diversity makes investments *stronger*, diversity can make relationships *weaker*. When you make this distinction, you see that relationships are dissimilar to investments when it comes to the effect of diversity. So the analogy is weak on the point of diversity.

When someone uses an analogy to persuade you about something, you need to recognize that an analogy is being used. Listen for words such as "like" or "the same as." These words indicate the person is comparing one thing with another and trying to make a connection. Then see if there are enough important similarities for the analogy to be strong and persuasive.

Albert Navarra

—The Key—

Strong, persuasive analogies have several important similarities;
weak ones don't.

Don't Assume the Traditional Way Is Still the Best Way

"WE'VE ALWAYS DONE it this way." That may be true. But should we *keep* doing it this way? That's what you should ask when someone makes an argument based on tradition.

Traditions exist in every part of life, for example medicine, marriage, culture, and business. And traditions are often beneficial. After all, it probably would not have become a tradition if it didn't work well at some point in time. Tradition is also familiar and comforting, while change is unfamiliar and uncomfortable.

The question is whether the tradition still works today. Have circumstances changed? Should adaptations be made? Would a new approach be more effective? Female genital mutilation, also known as female circumcision, is practiced in many countries. It's a tradition. But should it continue just because it's a tradition? Neckties are traditionally worn by men, not women. So should women never wear a necktie? Marriage has traditionally been between opposite sex couples. Should it stay like that, simply because it's always been so? Traditional thought was that the Earth was flat, that the Earth was the center of the universe, and that lobotomies were a good way to treat psychiatric problems. Should those traditions have continued, simply because they were traditions?

Any tradition must be based on today's facts, not yesterday's. So look for reasons and facts, *apart from tradition,* to support the argument. It may be that the tradition should continue because the reasons for the tradition still hold true today and nothing relevant or important has changed. Or it may be that the tradition should change because the facts have changed.

—THE KEY—

Traditional practices and beliefs must be justified by today's facts, not yesterday's.

Don't Put on Blinders

"I DON'T CARE what you say. I'm not going to change my mind." Really? So no matter what new facts or evidence you provide, the person's opinion will not change? Sometimes people get so caught up in their argument that they ignore any new facts, evidence, or reasons that go against their argument. They put on blinders, so to speak.

The Federal Drug Administration (FDA) approves a drug to treat depression, believing it is safe. Later, studies show the drug has serious, adverse side effects that were not known when the drug was first approved. Should the FDA ignore the new evidence and continue to approve the drug? An airline designs a new model of aircraft and puts it into service. Later, the airline learns that the electrical system sometimes overheats and catches fire. Should the airline refuse to acknowledge a problem with the electrical system?

Ignoring new information can be dangerous and lead to bad decisions. When you see someone "putting on blinders," ask if there is *any* evidence that would change this person's opinion. At this point, your goal is not so much to seek agreement; you just want to know if the other person is rational and open-minded. If the person says there is no fact, reason, or evidence that would change his or her mind, give it up. When a person's mind is made up, you might as well move on to something else.

—THE KEY—

Don't ignore new information; at least consider it.

Consider Alternatives

"YOU'RE EITHER FOR abortion or you're not." "You either support the right to bear arms or you don't." "You either love me or you don't." People sometimes make "black and white" arguments. It's either one thing or another. There are only two alternatives, and one of them must be correct.

But not all issues are "black and white." Sometimes there are shades of gray. One could be against abortion, but allow exceptions if necessary to protect the life or health of the mother. One could support the right to bear arms, but not for the mentally ill or in government buildings. You can give someone constructive criticism and still love the person.

"Black and white" arguments also appear when discussing possible solutions to a problem. "We should either engage in full-scale war or do nothing." There are other alternatives between conventional full-scale war and doing nothing. Military action can be limited in scope and duration. Human involvement can be limited with information technology, guidance systems, drones, and missiles.

In some cases, there may be only two options. But don't just assume that, or let someone else assume that, without thinking about it. At least explore whether there are any other reasonable alternatives.

Sometimes you can exercise multiple options at the same time. Research funding is a good example. There's a long-standing debate whether research should be funded publicly with taxpayer money or privately by companies. The debate often focuses on which is better, one or the other. But private companies sometimes avoid funding research unless they think it will be profitable. That leaves a gap that public funding can fill. So perhaps both public and private funding can be used for certain research projects.

—THE KEY—
Consider alternatives.

Don't Argue in a Circle

"THE MORAL THING for government to do is to prohibit obscenity on the Internet, because it is unconscionable to allow such sleazy and perverted material to proliferate on the Internet. It's just not right to allow obscene material to be published on the Internet."

Feeling a little dizzy? That's because the argument goes around in a circle. If you're half-paying attention, it might seem persuasive. But if you look more closely, you'll see the flaw. The argument simply says, *"It's the moral thing to do because it's the moral thing to do."* The argument assumes it's immoral to allow Internet obscenity, without giving any facts or reasons why. You can't just restate your point and call it an argument!

"Eat your veggies."

"Why?"

"Because I said so!" Sorry, Mom, but you're arguing in a circle. "Cornwell is definitely the best applicant for the job because she is a better applicant than the others." So, she's the best because she's the best?

These "circular" arguments are short. But let's say you come across a really long argument. Can a long argument be circular? Absolutely! If the "reasons" in the argument just restate the conclusion, then it's a circular argument and not persuasive.

—The Key—

Look out for "reasons" that are really recycled "conclusions."

A Team of All-Stars Is Not Always the Best Team

A PRADA DRESS with Gucci shoes and a Hermes bag doesn't guarantee a great look. Each product may be the industry best. But a great look depends on how a particular dress, pair of shoes, and bag look *together*. It's the combination of particular colors, shapes, textures, and other qualities that make an outfit look hot, or not.

You're staffing an office. You plan to recruit the best employees from your competitors, assuming you'll end up with a great office. And maybe you will. But it's not a sure bet. The "all-star" employees may have excelled in other offices, but the real test is how they work together *in your office*. You might end up with an office full of egos, too many leaders and not enough followers, and too much directing and not enough acting.

The owner of a sports team spends millions of dollars to sign several superstar players from other teams. Expectations are high. A team full of Hall of Fame players—they have to win, right? Sports fans know the answer to this one.

Cosmetic surgery can improve appearance and self-esteem. But there is risk in assuming that more "perfect" parts will make a more beautiful whole. You've probably seen people who have had Botox treatment, lip and breast augmentation, eye surgery, and maybe a few other procedures, and for some reason they don't look right. There is something uneven, disjointed, and sometimes even freakish about their appearance. Then there are other people whose features are flawed in some respect, but still look beautiful. Sometimes the parts don't need to be "perfect." They just need to fit together well and look "right." The ancient Greeks called this *symmetria*. Great parts don't always make a great whole.

—THE KEY—
Don't assume that a collection of great things
will be a great collection.

Don't Assume Each Part
Is the Same as the Whole

"I DON'T UNDERSTAND how they can expect to sell luxury tower condos for $10 million each when the average household income is $50,000! It doesn't make sense." This argument assumes that because the average household income of the *whole* country is $50,000, then the income of *each* household is also $50,000. But what's true of the whole is not always true of each individual part. Some households surely have $50,000 income. But some households have lower income. And other households have much higher income. So some households can afford those condos.

"Jason worked for a very prestigious university for many years, so I'm sure he would be a great hire for us." Makes sense, doesn't it? It's certainly not a bad thing that Jason worked for a great university for a long time. But what's the problem with this argument? What does it assume, without any analysis? The argument assumes that because the university is great, so is Jason. But what's true of the whole is not always true for each of the parts. The hiring decision would be better informed and more rational with more information on Jason and less about the university.

—THE KEY—

Don't assume that each part shares the qualities of the whole.

Rich Doesn't Always Mean Right

SO THERE'S THIS really rich guy. He owns villas and mansions all over the world. He has a warehouse of exotic cars. He travels extensively. And that's after he gives half his money to charity. You overhear him talking about the stock market at a coffee shop. He says to someone, "If I were you, I would buy XYZ stock." Do you trust his recommendation because he's rich? Many people would. Rich people have a certain aura in society. And it's assumed, sometimes, that wealthy people are more correct, intelligent, wise, or virtuous in some way. But that's not a reliable assumption. People can be very wealthy, and very corrupt or stupid. You have no idea how this guy made his money. Maybe he inherited it. Or maybe he created a smartphone app that finds fair trade, organic, vegan pastry shops anywhere in the world and sold it for $500 million dollars. Or maybe he's a crook. Does that mean his stock recommendation is solid?

Is a highly profitable company necessarily more virtuous? Is a wealthy country necessarily more virtuous? Not necessarily. Companies can show high profit without doing anything particularly virtuous. Countries can be wealthy and not show much regard for human rights or the environment.

You give a friend some business advice. Your friend isn't too crazy about your advice. But instead of examining your argument, he says, "If your business advice is so great, why aren't you rich?" How do you respond? First, notice that your friend attacked you instead of your argument; you know to focus his attention away from you and towards your argument. But your friend also assumes that rich is "right," and that not rich is "not right." Explain that advice from a rich person is not correct simply because the person's rich, and that advice from a person who is not rich is not wrong simply because the person is not rich. There are many people who are exceptionally intelligent and wise, yet not exceptionally wealthy.

—THE KEY—
Rich does not always mean "right."

Poor Doesn't Always Mean Wise

POVERTY IS A terrible condition that causes great sympathy. Mahatma Gandhi once said, "There are people in the world so hungry, that God cannot appear to them except in the form of bread." But poverty does not necessarily make a person's opinions stronger, or the person more virtuous. So a poor person's opinion on general matters, such as politics, economics, health, or education, does not carry more weight than a middle class person's opinion (or a rich person's opinion). So it should be assessed using the same factors used to assess any other person's opinion.

A poor person would, however, be a good source of facts about the circumstances of being poor. And if enough poor persons were surveyed, one could eventually have a large enough sample size to make reasonable generalizations about the poor.

—The Key—
Poverty does not necessarily
make a person's opinion stronger on general topics.

158

Big Arguments Need Small Goals

EATING A BIG meal takes a lot of small bites. Big arguments work the same way. They take time, and they proceed step by step.

You're trying to persuade your company to market a product in a foreign country. The company thinks you're crazy. The investment, logistics, and risks are huge. "Forget it," say the higher-ups. You need to cut up the argument and make some small goals. First prove there is demand for the product. Do research, visit the foreign country, and talk to people. If there is no current demand, show how demand can be generated, for example, with the right marketing, advertising, and pricing. When you have your evidence, make the "smaller" argument that there is, or will be, demand for the product. If your evidence is reliable, you will have an easier time convincing the company that there is demand for the product. And there is less risk for the company to agree with you on this one small point. Then you can move on to the next point.

Your next "bite" or point could be that the product can be delivered for a reasonable cost in a reliable manner. Gather your evidence and make your argument. If you persuade the company on this point, or at least get the company to have an open mind about it, then move on to the next. If you have the evidence to support your points, you can build a convincing case, step by step, for marketing the product abroad.

This strategy applies to any complex argument. Break it down into smaller points. Then argue one point at a time, until you've made them all. Then sum it up and show how it all fits together. If you have all your evidence and you have the time, you may be able to cover all the points in one meeting. Otherwise, it may take a series of meetings and discussions over a period of time. In that case, your goal is to make progress by making the "smaller" points at each meeting.

—The Key—
Win big arguments one small point at a time.

Entitlements

"I'M ENTITLED to my own opinion!" Frequent last words of some-one who is losing an argument and can't think of anything else to say. While it's true that everyone is entitled to have an opinion, everyone is not entitled to have the stronger opinion. But be careful. If you think you have the stronger argument and the other person says, "Well, I'm entitled to my opinion," respond by saying, "Absolutely, and I respect your opinion." Say it, and *mean it*, no matter how weak their argument is. Do not attack the person's dignity, and do not make it personal. If you do, the other person will become unnecessarily defensive and you'll make agreement more difficult.

Later, you can review why you think your argument is stronger, focusing on facts and reasons. By not attacking the person's dignity, you put the other person at ease, making it easier for them to reconsider the facts and reasons, and maybe, eventually, agree with you.

—THE KEY—
Respect people's right to their own opinion
and do not attack their dignity.

Don't Fall for Fancy Terms

FANCY TERMS CAN sound impressive. So they are frequently used, and sometimes abused, in argument. When that happens, people end up believing things that aren't true, or just confused.

First, a term, by itself, is not an argument. You'll often hear politicians use a term to describe something and just repeat it like an annoying robot. "This law will *decimate* national defense. If this bill becomes law it will simply *decimate* our armed forces." "The Court's decision is simply judicial *tyranny*. I'm tired of activist courts engaging in judicial *tyranny*." They act as if they're making an argument, but they're really just cheerleading. A real argument doesn't simply repeat a term; it makes a point and backs it up with reasons or facts.

You'll also hear people "argue by jargon," especially if they're selling something. They'll use fancy technical terms or buzzwords to make their argument or presentation sound impressive. A tech salesperson might use computer jargon, or a businessperson might use fancy corporate terms. If you don't understand a term, say so. Then distinguish between terms that are truly useful in explaining something and terms that are just BS and used to impress.

I heard a radio interview of a man who was tried for rape and murder. He said an expert witness testified at trial that hair evidence at the crime scene "matched" him. The expert witness used a lot of scientific language, technical words, and other fancy talk. The jury didn't really understand what the expert said, but the jury was "mesmerized" by the expert's words and the way he spoke. The man was convicted, said goodbye to his 12-year-old daughter, and began serving his sentence of life in prison. About eleven years later, the man was released from prison when it was shown that the hair evidence was unreliable. Had the jury looked beyond the expert's fancy words, might the jury also have concluded that the hair evidence was unreliable, all those years ago?

—THE KEY—
Don't be persuaded by fancy words.

Don't Cheat
on the Meaning of Terms

TERMS CAN BE helpful as symbols or shortcuts. But they must be used carefully. First, terms must be defined as clearly as possible. General, abstract terms should be made more specific and concrete. Otherwise you'll end up spending a lot of time arguing about something that is very subjective and hard to define. For example, before discussing the "best" movie ever, explain what you mean by "best." The same goes for any other generic term, for example, good, bad, fair, unfair, healthy, or unhealthy.

Also, after a term is used, don't change its meaning just for the sake of winning an argument. If you really need to clarify something, do it. But don't cheat on terms. The hiring manager says to a job applicant, "You've never held a leadership position, so I'm not sure you have the experience required for this management position."

"Actually, I was an Army Captain in Afghanistan and I was in command of more than 100 men for 15 months."

"I meant leadership in the private sector."

This job applicant has significant leadership experience under any reasonable definition of the term. There is no need to redefine leadership here. So if the company is looking for more private sector experience, then the question is private sector experience, not leadership.

—The Key—
Don't change the meaning of a term just to win an argument.

Distinguish Quantity
from Quality

A PRODUCT OR SERVICE claims to be 99% effective in stopping something unpleasant. You can use your imagination of unpleasant things. It sounds impressive—99%. That's a pretty high quantity of success. But what about the 1% that gets through? What if that 1% of unpleasant things is of such a quality that it is worse than the 99% of things that are avoided? Maybe the 99% of unpleasant things are just unpleasant, but the 1% is fatal. Then is a 99% success rate so great?

If an Ebola hazmat suit covers 99% of the body but leaves 1% uncovered, would you wear it? If an airbag deploys 99% of the time, would you want it in your car? If a parachute deploys 99% of the time, would you use it?

—THE KEY—
Consider quality as well as quantity
when looking at numbers in arguments.

Leave Your Wishes
by the Wishing Well

A MANAGER MAY wish for someone to be a good employee. But if the person is making a lot of mistakes that are hurting the company, then the company needs to take action. Just wishing and doing nothing will hurt the company.

You may wish that a person would be a good partner for you. But if the person is selfish and doesn't pay much attention to you, then the person is probably not going to be a good partner for you, no matter how much you wish for it.

You may wish for your 401(k) to stop losing money and start making money. But if your 401(k) is not invested in a diverse selection of quality investments, your wishes may go unfulfilled.

It's fine to wish for something, or against something. Other people have wishes too. But don't let your wishes or someone else's wishes control the argument. Wishing doesn't make anything true or false, probable or not probable. Always look at facts and reasons.

—THE KEY—
Wishing doesn't make it so.

167

Pity

SOMETIMES EMOTIONS are a good reason for doing something. Maybe you see someone in need and you feel pity, so you decide to help the person. That's the better part of being human. But pity can lead to bad decisions if it overrides other factors that are more important.

If you are responsible for hiring, and you hire someone not because of their qualifications, but because you are sympathetic to their personal circumstances, you may harm your company. Emotions are not a good reason for action in this case. If you work for border security at an international border, and you suspect that a traveler has a serious communicable disease, but you let the person through because you have pity for them, you may endanger the health of many others. If you are a teacher, and one of your students is failing tests, but you give the student a passing grade because you have pity for him, you may be hurting the student.

If you want to do something for purely emotional reasons and not rational reasons, you can. But be honest with yourself about what you are doing and the risks involved.

—THE KEY—
Be mindful of when emotions are a good reason for action
and when they are not.

Hot Words

"HOT WORDS" ARE so prejudicial and inflammatory that they should be avoided in arguments. You will find these words in society (racist, bigot, homophobe), in politics (fascist, communist, socialist), and in economics (crony capitalism, vulture capitalist). Dictators, recognizing the almost narcotic effect of hot words, use them as a propaganda tool to demonize opponents and control public opinion. Later, when society sobers up, they use the *names* of the dictators as hot words to attack current politicians. ("He is like Stalin.") Eventually, it's enough to simply use the hot word *dictator* to criticize a politician. ("He's like a dictator.")

The people who use hot words change over time. The hot words themselves change over time. And new hot words are occasionally born. But you can always recognize one when you hear it, if you're paying attention.

When used with people of the same mind, hot words tend to rally and affirm common feelings. But this is more cheerleading than argument. When hot words are used with an audience that disagrees, all hope for persuasion is lost. Hot words won't convince. They simply antagonize.

—THE KEY—

Avoid hot words.

Firsts

DON'T ASSUME SOMETHING is right or wrong simply because it has never been seen as right or wrong before. The smartest people on the planet once thought that Earth was flat, that heavy objects fall faster than lighter objects, that mercury should be widely used in medicine, and many other things that were later shown to be in error. Sometimes humans just get it wrong for a while, until someone comes along to set us straight. So don't be intimidated by consensus of opinion, or the fact that something has never been done, or never viewed a certain way. If you believe something is true, prove it, using facts and reason.

—THE KEY—
There are sometimes "firsts."

New and Improved!

YOU'VE SEEN THIS pitch plenty. Gaudy banners on buildings announce new ownership. Splashy labels on food products proclaim "New and Improved!" Guru authors hype a new paradigm in economics, education, technology, or existence itself. The moment people see "new," they think "better." But it's not so simple.

The first question is whether anything has really changed. So what if a restaurant has new ownership? All that means to me is that a different person is making money. Unless the food, service, prices, or decor changes, nothing has really changed that affects me.

The second question is whether the change is better. I heard a story about a yogurt company that put less yogurt in the cups, leaving a gap at the top, at the same price, and marketed it as "new and improved" because the extra room made it easier to sprinkle stuff on top. Would you consider that better?

Every few years, new politicians are elected. A few years later, the electorate is completely fed up with those politicians and giddily looking forward to the next election of "new" ones. Should we be encouraged?

—THE KEY—
"New" is not automatically better.

Drawing the Line

A SALESPERSON TRIES to sell you something by saying you can make monthly payments. You say you already have a lot of monthly expenses, and really can't afford more. The salesperson says it will cost only an extra $9.95 a month. Tempted?

You're trying to lose weight, so you're counting calories. You've already consumed your caloric limit for the day, when someone offers you a very high quality piece of imported chocolate. You have to try it, they say. What to do?

Many arguments are based on the idea that one more step really doesn't matter that much. It's just a "matter of degree." So go ahead and do it. A few more dollars, a few more calories, one more drink. But sometimes it is important to draw a line somewhere. Exactly where the line is drawn may seem a bit arbitrary at times. But if you are trying to accomplish something, having a line is better than not. Avoiding bankruptcy is easier if you set spending limits for yourself. Losing weight is easier if you set caloric limits. Promoting highway safety is easier with speed limits.

—THE KEY—

Sometimes you have to draw the line.

You Did Too!

YOU HAVE A FRIEND who spends all her income on food, enter-tainment, clothes, and travel, and saves nothing. Then one day she tells you, "You should set aside some money for your old age. Maybe set up an IRA or something."

"Easy for you to say," you reply.

Your aunt never married. One day she tells you, "You should think about getting married, having kids. Don't be afraid."

"Aunty, you never even got engaged," you say.

It's natural to examine the person along with the argument they make. But that's an *emotional* response, not a rational one. Your friend argues that saving some money is good for *you*. Whether she saves has no bearing on the wisdom of saving. She's making a point, and if you disagree, you should explain why, rather than attack your friend.

Your aunt argues that marriage and family tend to make life happier and more fulfilling, as it may for you. The argument stands or falls on its own merits, regardless of whether aunty ever married.

Responding to an argument by saying "you did it too" is faulty because it changes the subject and introduces a new argument to the discussion, namely, that there is something wrong with the other person.

If someone responds to an argument you make by saying "you do it too," admit it, if it's true. Say, "That's right!" Then redirect the person's attention to your argument, and away from you. This will help the other person realize that your personal history is irrelevant, and that the reasons in support of your claim are more important.

—THE KEY—
Don't point fingers.

Challenge Authorities

PACKAGING FOR A dental product says "leading dentists" recommend it. But why? A recommendation, without facts and reasons, is just a conclusion, not an argument. A reporter cites "unnamed sources" for a story that a politician may have committed a crime. But an accusation, without facts, is just a claim. And anybody can claim anything.

Sometimes experts give opinions on complex subjects. But you should, as much as possible, see if you can understand the facts upon which the expert bases his or her opinion and reasoning. Medicine is a good example. A doctor recommends surgery for you. This is essentially an argument that you should agree to surgery. But why? What diagnostic testing was done? What did it show? How will surgery help? What is the probable outcome? You should at least ask and try to understand these things so you can judge the strength of your doctor's recommendation for surgery. And you can also get a second or third opinion from other doctors and let them assess or challenge the first doctor's opinion.

Celebrities often endorse products and services. But is the celebrity an expert in the field? Did the celebrity have access to the facts necessary for a sound opinion? Should you make your purchasing decision based solely on the celebrity's endorsement?

—THE KEY—

Challenge "expert" opinions and don't accept them at face value.

Two-Second Logic Test

HERE'S A QUICK, simple, and often effective test. Someone makes an argument that something is good or bad. For example, "*Homosexuality* should be illegal because it is unnatural." Replace the key term, "homosexuality," with something the other person accepts should be legal, like anesthesia. "So would you argue that *anesthesia* should be illegal, because it also is unnatural?" You immediately undercut the heart of the argument that something should be illegal solely because it is unnatural.

"*Marriage* should be only between a man and a woman, because it has always been so."

"So would you have argued that *slavery* should not have been abolished in the United States, because until the 13th Amendment it had "always been so"?

—THE KEY—

Replace the key term in an argument with another term,
and see if the argument still makes sense.

181

Symbols

SYMBOLS REPRESENT THINGS and ideas, and they can be very powerful. For example, logos and trademarks are symbols, and they instantly communicate various qualities of a product or service. Symbols typically act as a shortcut to communicate something that would otherwise take many words.

There are no shortcuts to good argument, yet people sometimes use symbols in an effort to persuade. When a financial advisor speaks to you wearing a suit, the suit is a symbol. So is his watch, cologne, car, and even the office in which he sits, with its expensive furnishings and expansive views. The advisor hopes these things will represent that he is successful, trustworthy, and competent, and will help him persuade you. But do these things matter? If the advisor dressed in a shabby manner and worked in the back of a frozen yogurt shop, one might wonder if he is a serious professional. So to some extent, these things do matter. Certain standards and uniformities are expected from professionals.

So are these things enough? You would never want to make a

significant financial decision based solely on the advisor's clothing and accessories. An investment decision should be based on several factors, for example, financial needs, appetite for risk, and time horizon—an *argument*, in other words. And symbols alone are not an argument.

Some public figures often wear certain clothing, at least in public. A political activist might wear a baseball cap as a symbol to represent himself as a "man of the people." A politician might wear a flag pin on his suit lapel to symbolize that he is a patriot. A company president might wear T-shirts as a symbol to represent that she relates to a certain demographic of people. Be careful not to take these symbols as arguments. They are no different than the financial advisor's tie. They're just symbols.

—THE KEY—
A symbol is not an argument.

Second Thoughts

PEOPLE CHANGE THEIR minds for different reasons. Sometimes it's just caving, purely a sign of weakness. Relentless opposition or fear of negative consequences can cause one to change positions. Sometimes it's done for expediency, or to win favor with a particular group of people. Politicians, for example, are routinely criticized for "flip-flopping," "waffling," or switching sides on important issues. And sometimes the person who changes his or her mind is proven right in the end, even when the motive for changing positions was less than admirable!

So before you change your mind on a topic, or criticize others for changing their mind, look deeper than motive. Consider whether a change of position is justified by new information, new consequences, or a new way of analyzing the situation. Forget about motives for a moment and reexamine the argument.

New, relevant facts can justify a change of position. In some situations, refusing to change positions in the face of new facts would be stupid. For example, general medical practices are frequently revised when new information is revealed. Lobotomies were a popular form of treatment for mental illness for many years. The neurophysician who developed the procedure even won the Nobel Prize for Physiology or Medicine. But when better forms of treatment were developed, for example medicines, lobotomies fell out of favor. New facts changed medical opinion.

Sometimes better analysis can justify changing an opinion. Maybe you just got it wrong the first time you considered the issue. You made an error in reasoning. If you open your mind and realize the other person has the better argument, and you are free to change your mind, consider doing so. Why stick to a losing argument?

If you decide to change your mind, explain thoroughly why you changed your mind. If someone objects to your change of position, focus the other person's attention on the reasons why you changed your mind, not simply on the fact that you changed positions. Similarly, if you object to someone changing a position on an issue, ask for an explanation. Look beyond motive. Examine the substance of the argument.

—THE KEY—
New facts or better analysis
may justify a change of position on an issue.

Stubbornness

NEW INFORMATION or better analysis sometimes justifies a change of position. Yet you (or the other person) refuse to change. Why? There are many reasons why people sometimes resist changing their mind on an issue, even in the face of overwhelming evidence.

Some don't want to admit they were wrong in the first place. Others may fear being ostracized from a group if they change their position. And sometimes people become "married" to a position and just don't want to let go. They identify themselves with their position so much that changing positions would be like changing themselves and becoming a different person.

But truth is powerful. It usually wins out in time. So if circumstances warrant it, consider changing positions and getting on the winning side. And monitor yourself (or the other person) to see if you have become more concerned with "winning" the argument or protecting your ego than being correct.

There are several ways to deal with a stubborn opponent. Focus the person's attention on the truth or substance of the argument and away from him- or herself. Reassure the person that in the long run, it is better to be correct than consistent. This is what Ralph Waldo Emerson meant when he wrote, "A foolish consistency is the hobgoblin of little minds."

For the person who has fused his ego to his position, disassociate the person from the position. Avoid making the argument personal. Avoid using the word "you" during discussions. Make it clear that you do not measure the person by the position. You just want to get the issue right.

—The Key—
Correct is better than consistent.

Don't Insult

IT FEELS GOOD to hurl an insult sometimes. Sometimes it feels *great*. But when you argue, you want more than temporary good feelings. You argue for important, lasting reasons. So don't ruin your chance of success by insulting the other person. You know an insult when you see one, but here are some of the most tempting.

- "Are you *nuts?*" (and variations like *high, crazy, kidding, joking*).
- "Ask anyone and they'll tell you…" (and variations like *everybody knows, obviously, anyone can see*).
- "You are so wrong!" (also, *dead wrong, way off base, wrong-headed*).

Notice something about insults that is very common with weak arguments. They are not *relevant* to the argument. They do nothing to prove your point. Nor do they disprove your opponent's points. They're just "feel good" statements that pretty much destroy any chance you have of convincing another person you are right.

—The Key—

Instead of insulting the other person, attack the argument.

Don't Give Up!

WINSTON CHURCHILL ARGUED from 1929 to 1939 that Hitler's Germany was a growing danger that should be taken seriously. Churchill was adamant that appeasement of Hitler was not a viable solution. People called him a "warmonger" (*hot word*) and said he was just eager to go to war. On May 10, 1940, George VI appointed Churchill as prime minister. Hours later, the German Army invaded the Netherlands, Belgium and Luxembourg. Two days later the German Army invaded France.

Persistence pays off. If it's important, don't quit. Don't be discouraged if you don't reach a quick agreement. And don't be discouraged if the other person makes some great points or counterarguments. Take it as an opportunity to improvise, adapt, and overcome. You may need to give it a rest for a while, but don't quit! After letting some time pass, go after it again.

—THE KEY—
If it's important, be persistent.

Power of Pause

"TA-TA-TA-TAAA (pause) ta-ta-ta-Taaa." The famous opening of Beethoven's Symphony No. 5. It's so powerful and dramatic, not just for the notes, but the pause between them.

There is something similar in the visual arts known as negative space. This is the blank or white area around objects, which gives the eye a place to "rest," and thereby highlights the object. Think of the logo for Apple Inc., and how the negative space draws your eye towards the "bite" of the apple.

Argument can also make powerful use of silence. If the other person does not agree with you after a good amount of argument, consider giving it a rest for a while. The other person may have strong emotional and logical reasons for his or her opinion. Or the person may be completely nuts! Either way, sometimes it's not possible to overcome all obstacles in one discussion, or even several discussions. Some things take time. And if you keep hammering away you might just make the other person "dig in" and take an even more defensive posture. You may also damage a relationship or potential relationship.

So make your points, explain your reasons, and give the person something to think about. Then give the person time to think. This shows respect for the other person, and may buy you some goodwill when you pick up the discussion later. You may want to wait a few hours, days, weeks, or even months before picking up the argument again. Use your judgment, based on the nature of the obstacles to agreement.

—THE KEY—

Give the other person time and freedom to agree with you.

Audio- and Videoconferencing

IN AUDIOCONFERENCING, THE listeners can't see you, so the connection between you and others is weaker. But there are things you can do to minimize this problem.

First, call in early and try to be the first to call in. Being the first will help you stand out and give you the chance to introduce yourself to others in the conference call before the conference officially begins.

Second, speak a little slower than you do in person. This will help others understand your points and reasons.

Third, periodically confirm that the group understands key points. You don't have to ask if they agree. Just confirm they understand what you are saying.

Finally, provide a summary at the end to confirm anything that needs to be done in the future. For example, if certain information needs to be gathered or analyzed, say so at the end of the discussion.

Videoconferencing allows others to see you, enhancing the connection between you and your audience. But make sure you look your best. For example, the video camera should be approximately eye level as you look straight ahead. If your camera is in your laptop or tablet, and your device is too low, the camera will be pointing up at your face, and this may not be the most flattering view. So place something under your device to lift the camera to eye level.

Also make sure the lighting is good—not too dark and not too bright. And make sure to put your cell phone on vibrate and do what you can to eliminate outside noise. If you are in a room, put a sign on the door that says something like "PLEASE DO NOT DISTURB—CONFERENCE CALL IN PROGRESS."

Finally, if you are sharing documents via the Internet, make sure all the participants have the documents before you begin.

Be Classy

IT FEELS GOOD to win an argument. Actually, it feels great! But don't rub it in. Be a good sport about it. If the other person agreed with you reluctantly, gloating may cause the other person to change his or her mind. Celebrate the triumph of truth rather than the defeat of an opponent. Celebrate that you both agree on something, rather than celebrating your "victory" in a personal sense.

—THE KEY—
Respect the other person's dignity
and don't brag about winning an argument.

Index

Made in the USA
Middletown, DE
03 June 2023

31994381R00123